The Essential Guide to Short Sales and Avoiding Foreclosure in Pennsylvania

By Tai A. DeSa

I0479650

WARNING AND DISCLAIMER

This book is not legal advice.

This book is not legal advice. I am not an attorney, a tax advisor, or a certified credit counselor. Your attorney and accountant can advise you regarding your particular situation and how it is affected by your state's laws. This book is for informational purposes and should not be construed as legal advice. Every pre-foreclosure situation is different.

CONTENTS

PROLOGUE. WHO WROTE THIS BOOK AND WHY SHOULD I LISTEN TO THE AUTHOR?

One study indicated that as many as 70 percent of people facing foreclosure do nothing. (New York Times, 2008) That's right, nothing. They do not consult an attorney, or a real estate agent, or an accountant, or a certified credit counselor, a short sale negotiator, or anyone else who might be able to help them. They are too embarrassed, scared, confused, and frustrated. Please do not be part of that 70 percent. Read this book.

The best is always yet to come. I am here to tell you that even though you may be in the midst of a dark winter financially, know that spring is just around the corner. The night is darkest just before the dawn. Every problem we face is a gift, if only we embrace it that way. Problems test us and make us stronger and more appreciative of the good things in life. Even if you are in a tough financial position, know that it is only temporary. You are bigger than your house and your financial situation. And there are people out there who are willing to help you.

If you are a person who needs to sell a property but you owe more than it is worth, then this book will empower you to make better choices. I want you to know:

1. You have many more options than you think.

2. Now is the best time to sell a property via a short sale. The government and many banks created a number of helpful programs that did not exist just a few years ago.

3. Applied knowledge is power. By understanding what you can do, you put yourself in a position to relieve stress and make empowering decisions.

If you are a real estate agent, attorney, credit counselor, accountant, or anyone else looking to help a client avoid foreclosure, then you too will find this book valuable.

My name is Tai DeSa. I have been involved in hundreds of successful short sales since 2005. I am a licensed real estate broker in Pennsylvania and Tennessee, and I co-founded of one of the nation's leading short sale processing companies. I learned how to lead people through crises when I served as a U.S. Navy Officer in the Kosovo Campaign, the Global War on Terror, and the Iraq War. I hope to help lead you through your personal housing crisis. I learned about business at the

Wharton School at the University of Pennsylvania, and now I have made my business one of helping those who might not be helped by anyone else.

I wrote this book because thousands of Pennsylvanians owe more on their house than what it is worth. I have gone through three short sales myself, so I know first-hand the range of emotions that you may be experiencing.

My Promise to You

In this book, I will give you answers to more short sale questions than what most people ask. Allow me to help you close one chapter of your life and start a new, much better chapter. If you are a real estate agent or attorney working on a short sale, this book will equip you with specific knowledge to help you serve your client at the highest level. If you are a buyer or investor, you'll learn valuable tips that can help you set expectations and negotiate a good deal.

You do not have to read this book cover to cover like a novel. Feel free to jump straight to the sections that are most relevant to you.

Now, let's get things done. Read on!

CHAPTER 1. WHAT THE HECK ARE SHORT SALES AND FORECLOSURES ANYWAY?

Nothing in life is to be feared. It is only to be understood. Now is the time to understand more, so that we may fear less.

- Marie Curie

It was a sunny winter day in early 2006, and I was sitting with Joe in the lawyer's office. Joe, a man in his early 40s, was in the middle of a divorce. His wife and kids had moved out of their house. Joe was struggling to pay the bills. He knew he had to sell his house, and he did what other people normally do when they want to sell – Joe hired a real estate agent.

That agent found a buyer who was willing to pay $246,000 for the home. But there was a problem. A week before the settlement, the title agency calculated that the total balance of liens and fees for Joe was $259,000. In other words, Joe was $13,000 short. Joe literally had only a few dollars to his name, so he was not in a position to pay $13,000 to sell his house. The buyer became upset with Joe and terminated the real estate contract. The listing agent was so flustered that he canceled the listing, as he knew that the $246,000 offer was the highest the market would bear. To sell his house, Joe needed to have someone convince his three mortgage lenders to take less money.

The attorney was in his late 60s, sporting a suit and tie that had seen better years. This attorney was eccentric but one could tell he was brilliant. He perused Joe's financial documents and mortgage statements for several minutes while we waited in silence. Then the attorney looked up, and said, "Joe, stop making your mortgage payments. It's obvious you cannot afford this house anymore. There's no point in continuing to pay for something that has no value and creates all this stress for you."

The grizzled lawyer proceeded to instruct Joe to continue living in the house until we could find a buyer and negotiate a short sale approval from each of Joe's three mortgage lenders. The attorney predicted it would take about six months for everything to be negotiated. He told Joe that by not paying the mortgages, he could save up about $10,000 in those six months. That would be enough for Joe to start the next phase of his life.

4

Joe did just as he was instructed. This prescient lawyer was right on, as this particular short sale took six months to negotiate and sell. Each of Joe's mortgage lenders forgave the remaining debt, and Joe had enough money to start the next phase of his life. Today Joe is a successful businessman. That short sale is ancient history.

So What Is a Short Sale?

A short sale is a sale of mortgaged property where the proceeds from the sale are insufficient to pay in full the seller's outstanding mortgage and any other liens against the property *and* the seller lacks sufficient other assets to pay the remaining amounts due on the secured debts. Because the seller lacks the financial ability to remove these encumbrances in order to convey marketable and insurable title, the seller's lender and any other lienholders must consent to the sale and voluntarily release their liens.

If someone owes more on their house than what it is worth and they have a compelling reason to sell, then that person will need a short sale.

Example of a Short Sale

Fred and Sally purchased their home for $300,000 in 2006. They borrowed $285,000 via a purchase money mortgage. In 2012, Fred was laid off from his job and Sally had to cut her work hours to care for her ailing father. Since Fred and Sally fell behind on their mortgage, they asked a real estate agent to list their house. The agent reviewed comparable sales from the area which suggested that the house was valued about $250,000. The agent listed the house at $249,900 and soon received an offer for $245,000. Since Fred and Sally owed about $280,000 and the mortgage was in default, the lender eventually agreed to permit the sale for $245,000. The lender allowed the agent to receive a sales commission. Fred and Sally received no proceeds from the sale, but they were pleased to avoid an embarrassing foreclosure sale of their house.

Here are the numbers if there is no short sale:

$245,000	Sale price
- $ 14,700	6% real estate agent commission
- $ 2,450	1% Pennsylvania realty transfer tax
- $ 4,550	Closing costs and pro-rated property taxes
- $280,000	Mortgage payoff
$(56,700)	Shortfall that the seller is expected to pay

So, if Fred and Sally had $56,700 laying around and if they did not want to negotiate a short sale, they could simply bring that amount to the settlement to sell their house.

In most cases, people do not have the money to make up the difference. Even if they have the money, sometimes they may want to negotiate something with the lender anyway.

Here are the numbers if there is a short sale negotiated with Fred and Sally's lender:

	$245,000	Sale price
-	$ 14,700	6% real estate agent commission
-	$ 2,450	1% Pennsylvania realty transfer tax
-	$ 4,550	Closing costs and pro-rated property taxes
-	$223,300	Mortgage payoff, as the lender takes a $56,700 loss
	$ 0	Amount that the seller is expected to pay

In this case, Fred and Sally can sell their house without having to pay anything at settlement or owing any additional money after the sale.

Elements of a Successful Short Sale

1. The property is worth less than what is owed.

2. The seller has a hardship that makes it impractical for the seller to keep the property.

3. The seller is cooperative and willing to work with a real estate salesperson.

4. The lender is contacted and expresses willingness to consider a short sale.

5. A ready, willing, and able buyer can purchase the property in a timely manner.

What Is a Pre-Foreclosure?

A property in a pre-foreclosure status means that the underlying mortgage loan is delinquent but a foreclosure sale has not yet occurred. Not all short sales are pre-foreclosures, as some people are current on their mortgage but still need a short sale to sell their property.

Not all pre-foreclosures are short sales, either. If the property can be sold for an amount that pays off the liens in full, then no short sale is needed. The seller might even receive some of the proceeds of the sale.

Here are the numbers in a pre-foreclosure sale where the seller still has equity:

	$ 245,000	Sale price
-	$ 14,700	6% real estate agent commission
-	$ 2,450	1% Pennsylvania realty transfer tax
-	$ 4,550	Closing costs and pro-rated property taxes
-	$ 190,000	Mortgage balance, including late charges and fees
	$ 33,300	Amount that seller receives at settlement

If you are a property owner facing foreclosure and you have equity, these are your options:

1. Sell the property quickly before you lose your remaining equity. Tell your lender that you're in the process of selling the property, as some lenders may grant you a little more time with a forbearance plan.

2. Become current on the loan. You could enter into a forbearance plan or loan modification with the lender. Alternately, you could borrow enough money to bring the loan current.

> Forbearance: a policy of restraint in taking legal action to remedy a default or other breach of contract, generally in the hope that the default will be cured, given additional time. The lender or creditor may postpone or temporarily reduce payments.

3. Do nothing. The property will ultimately be foreclosed, and you will likely lose all your equity. Warning: do not try this at home!

What Is the Foreclosure Process?

Foreclosure is a legal process in which a mortgage lender claims real estate from a borrower who has failed to pay or who may have breached the loan agreement in some other way. When the owner borrowed money, they gave the lender a mortgage against the property as security for the loan. The owner is the mortgagor, and the lender is the mortgagee.

The foreclosure process varies among states. The type of procedure depends on whether the state uses deeds of trust or mortgages. Generally, states that use mortgages conduct judicial foreclosures. States that use deeds of trust conduct non-judicial foreclosures, using an out-of-court process. Pennsylvania is a judicial state.

Judicial Foreclosure

Judicial states require that a foreclosure go through the court system. Generally, states that use mortgages conduct judicial foreclosures. The bank must file a court action, typically a lawsuit, against the borrower. The process takes time, and it involves a sequence of events that takes months, even years, before the foreclosure process is complete. A judicial foreclosure process typically benefits the borrower, as it buys them time to find a solution or a new residence.

The judicial process involves the filing of a Complaint by the lender along with a Lis Pendens notice, which is a notice of pending legal action. The borrower is served notice of the Complaint, and they have an opportunity to be heard before the court if they wish. If the court finds that the debt is valid, a Default Judgment will be issued in favor of the lender, and it will list the entire unpaid balance plus late fees, legal fees, and court costs. After the Default Judgment is entered, a writ will be issued by the court authorizing a Sheriff's Sale. The Sheriff's Sale is a public auction open to anyone. The bank's attorney or representative may attend the sale, and the bank may either take the property back if the bids are not high enough, or the bank may allow the property to be sold to the highest bidder.

> Pennsylvania is a judicial foreclosure state. The mortgage lender must go through the court system to foreclose. The lender cannot simply take the property because the borrower missed some payments.

8

Non-Judicial Foreclosure

Other states, typically western states, utilize a non-judicial foreclosure process. A document called a deed of trust is created when the mortgage loan is granted. When a borrower fails to pay, the default starts the foreclosure process right away without having to go through the courts. The borrower has a certain period of time, which varies by state, to sell the property, pay the delinquent amount, or negotiate another solution.

In the case of a deed of trust, the deed to the property is held by a third party, or trustee. If the entire loan balance is paid, the trustee then transfers ownership interest via a trustee's deed or a reconveyance to the borrower.

If a borrower fails to pay, the lender instructs the trustee to sell the property. The trustee may be another bank, an escrow agent, or a title company. The third party orders a sale, which is open to the public and advertised in local newspapers. Typically a trustee's sale involves sealed bids. Even the mortgage lender submits a sealed bid. If their bid is highest, they become the new owner of the property.

The average time to foreclose on a property has increased across the country. Banks, courts, foreclosure attorneys, and Sheriff's Departments have become inundated. Borrowers are attempting loan modifications, forbearance plans, short sales, and other programs which typically delay the foreclosure process. Banks have sometimes delayed sales to maintain good public relations. For example, many banks choose to suspend foreclosure sales around Christmas. Other banks sometimes place a temporary moratorium on foreclosures due to complaints by borrowers, state governments, or others. In addition, an increasing number of borrowers choose to contest the foreclosure action against them, which delays the foreclosure sale.

Timeline for Foreclosure in Pennsylvania

January 1st	January mortgage payment due but not paid
February 1st	February mortgage payment also due. Two months' payments are now due.
March 1st	March mortgage payment due. Three months' payments are now due.

March 6th	Lis Pendens Notice. For residential properties, the lender must send an Act 91 Notice (Take Action to Save Your Home From Foreclosure). The lender may send an Act 6 Notice (Notice of Intent to Foreclosure) too. The homeowner has 20-30 days to respond to cure the default or rectify the situation in some other way if they wish to prevent a foreclosure lawsuit.
May 8th	The maximum 30 days in the Act 6 and Act 91 Notices are up. The lender hires a foreclosure attorney.
June 9th	The foreclosure attorney for the lender files a complaint at the county courthouse (Court of Common Pleas).
July 10th	The borrower fails to respond to the complaint, and a default judgment is entered in favor of the lender.
August 11th	The county Sheriff's office schedules a date for the Sheriff's Sale.
August 31st	A notice of the Sheriff's Sale is served to the borrower and sent to the other lien holders.
October 30th	The Sheriff's Sale is held.
November 13th	The Sheriff's office prepares and records a deed conveying title to the purchaser. If a third party did not purchase the property at the Sheriff's Sale, then the deed conveys title to the mortgage lender.
November 23rd	Eviction or Ejectment process begins if the borrower is still residing at the property.

Typically the foreclosure process in Pennsylvania will take longer than the above diagram. The lender may delay filing of a foreclosure lawsuit because they're inundated or because they are attempting a workout with the borrower. The borrower could delay the process with legal motions. The judge in the county court may delay the foreclosure process to see if the borrower and lender's attorney can reach a better solution. The Sheriff's Department may delay the sale because they're overwhelmed.

CHAPTER 2. MYTHS AND TRUTHS ABOUT SHORT SALES

The trouble with life isn't that there is no answer, it's that there are so many answers.

- Ruth Benedict

Myth: A person must be behind on their payments to sell their house as a short sale.

Truth: Many mortgage lenders are considering short sales even when the borrower is current on their payments.

Myth: If a person sells their house as a short sale, they will owe money to their lender.

Truth: In many short sales, the lender forgives the remaining debt.

Myth: Short sales are only allowed for owner-occupied homes.

Truth: Short sales are permitted on commercial buildings, investment properties, land, and any other type of real estate.

Myth: An owner can sell their property as a short sale without listing with an agent.

Truth: Mortgage lenders want to know that a real estate agent listed the property and marketed it to the general public, so a reasonable and ethical offer is generated.

Myth: You need a buyer before the lender will negotiate a short sale.

11

Truth: More and more lenders and short sale programs are considering pre-approvals before a bona fide buyer offer is presented.

Myth: In a short sale, the lender owns the house.

Truth: The homeowner is the owner of record until the property is transferred, so in a short sale the lender does not take ownership unless a foreclosure occurs.

Myth: The lender is responsible for property maintenance.

Truth: The owner of record is responsible and liable for the property, so they must shovel the snow, cut the grass, keep the pipes from freezing, and maintain insurance coverage.

Myth: There are laws that require lenders to respond to short sale offers from buyers in a certain period of time.

Truth: There are no laws that require lenders to respond to offers, but there are some short sale programs where participating lenders agree to respond under certain conditions.

Myth: All short sales follow the same timeline.

Truth: Each short sale varies, depending upon the lender, the short sale program, whether there is a buyer, and how responsive the seller is to lender requests for paperwork.

Myth: The lender always forgives the remaining debt.

Truth: While many lenders forgive the remaining debt, some lenders may expect a contribution from the seller or perhaps a promissory note to be paid later.

Myth: The lender can be convinced not to send an IRS Form 1099-C to the borrower.

Truth: In all short sales involving forgiven debt, the lender sends a 1099 to the former borrower as a means of writing off their loss.

Myth: One person at the lender can make the decision to approve a short sale.

Truth: In most short sales, there are a series of decision-makers, including people at the servicer, the investor, the mortgage insurer, and a government entity.

Myth: Calling the lender every day makes a short sale happen faster.

Truth: Successful short sales often involve periods of intense activity followed by periods of inactivity, where one must wait for another party to run through their process.

Myth: The lender will delay a foreclosure action if an offer was sent to them.

Truth: Some lenders will delay a foreclosure action in some cases, but they often will continue with the foreclosure even while considering a short sale.

CHAPTER 3. THE CAST OF CHARACTERS IN THE SAGA OF THE SHORT SALE

Debt, we've learned, is the match that lights the fire of every crisis. Every crisis has its own set of villains – pick your favorite: bankers, regulators, central bankers, politicians, overzealous consumers, credit rating agencies – but all require one similar ingredient to create a true crisis: too much leverage.

- Andrew Ross Sorkin

This book addresses short sales and foreclosures from the perspective of the seller, listing agent, buyer's agent, buyer, and mortgage lender/servicer. Each party has a different stake in the transaction. However, keep this in mind. In a traditional real estate transaction it is seller versus buyer, often with real estate agents in between to keep the negotiation reasonable, civil, and productive. In a short sale, it is more like seller, buyer, and agents versus the seller's mortgage lender. If the seller receives no money from the sale of the property, then their motivation is not to make more money as is often the case in a traditional sale. Short sales often require a true team effort from the parties so they can achieve a common goal.

The Players in a Short Sale Transaction

Below are the cast of characters in the saga of the short sale.

- *Seller(s)*. They are also referred to as the Borrower or Homeowner.

- *Lender(s)*. These are the banks or investors with liens against the property. In many cases, the loan may have been sold from one lender to another. In other cases, a loan servicer may be handling the collection of payments for the lender.

- *Loss Mitigation Officers*. The loss mitigation specialists or negotiators of a lender or servicer help determine an acceptable payoff.

- *Real Estate Agent(s)*. Typically the property will be listed with a real estate licensee. Another agent may represent the prospective buyer.

14

- *Short Sale Consultant or Negotiator.* There are many legitimate and experienced short sale consultants who act as a third party liaison or negotiator to help sellers and agents. There are also many illegitimate or inexperienced people claiming to be short sale consultants. Having a professional consultant work the short sale can make or break a deal.

- *Contractor(s) and Inspector(s).* Many distressed properties are devalued by deferred maintenance or neglect. An estimate from a licensed contractor and a report from a certified inspector may be powerful negotiating tools in convincing a lender to accept less money.

- *Appraiser or BPO Agent.* The lender or servicer will likely pay for an appraisal or a Broker's Price Opinion (BPO) from an agent. The lender will determine a payoff based upon the valuation established by the appraiser or BPO agent. It is imperative that the listing agent and/or short sale consultant communicate with the appraiser or BPO agent to explain the nature of the transaction.

- *Attorney(s).* The lender or servicer will hire a law firm to represent them in the foreclosure action. The seller is strongly encouraged to have legal representation too. The buyer might even have a lawyer represent them, although it is not necessary in Pennsylvania.

- *Accountant(s).* The seller is strongly encouraged to consult with their accountant in any short sale or potential short sale transaction.

> TAI TIDBITS...
>
> Just because someone at the lender or servicer tells you something does not mean that it is entirely accurate. Countless times I have heard homeowners tell me, "The bank said this" or "The bank told me that." It was really a low-level clerk at the bank who read something from a script that the homeowner or agent interpreted as the undisputed truth. If you don't like what you hear, call back and speak with someone else. Or escalate to a supervisor.

- *Credit Restoration Specialist or Counselor.* The seller is strongly encouraged to speak with a credit counselor prior to a short sale transaction. After a short sale, it may be a good idea for the seller to hire a credit restoration service to help clean up their damaged credit record.

CHAPTER 4. BENEFITS OF A SHORT SALE

You may not realize it when it happens, but a kick in the teeth may be the best thing in the world for you.

- Walt Disney

It is important to understand the benefits of a short sale to each of the parties involved. Why would a seller want to cooperate? Why would a lender accept less than what is owed? Why would a buyer want to wait for a short sale to be approved? Why would an agent take on the potential headache of a short sale? Why would anyone subject themselves to such pain and disappointment?

How Sellers Benefit

- *Closure.* People facing foreclosure are inundated with collection calls, threatening letters, and visits from the county sheriff's deputies. They no longer want to answer the phone or doorbell, and they dread walking to the mailbox to check the mail. Selling a property before a final foreclosure action brings the unpleasant calls, letters, and visits to an end. The seller can move on with their life.

- *Dignity.* Imagine the shame of having sheriff's deputies forcibly move you out of what was once your home. Imagine the awkward looks of the neighbors as you hurriedly throw a handful of possessions into a waiting car or truck. Imagine seeing the lender's locksmith changing the locks as you leave the property for the final time. A short sale allows the seller to have a normal

> TAI TIDBITS...
>
> If you cannot afford to pay for your house and it has negative equity, then at a certain point you have to make a business decision. Every dollar you spend on an upside-down house is a dollar you will not get back. It may make sense to save up your money for the next stage of your life while you work with a real estate agent to sell your property.

closing and a move on their own schedule. In most cases, the neighbors won't know that a seller sold their property via a short sale.

- *Credit.* A short sale, while damaging to a person's credit, is less damaging than allowing the property to go to foreclosure.[1] Settling the debt and ending the delinquent payments allows a person to stop the damage and start rebuilding their credit sooner. It is important to note that a short sale may affect a borrower's credit for up to seven years but usually less, because lenders might report that a loan was settled for less than its balance. A seller may be able to convince the lender to include a letter of explanation in the credit file that outlines the extenuating circumstances that caused the short sale. This can soften the blow to one's credit.[2] It's important to remember that a short sale is a temporary setback, whereas a foreclosure has permanence in some respects.

- *Prevent a Deficiency Judgment.* If the seller opts for a deed-in-lieu of foreclosure, they might surrender the property without an agreement on the lender's loss. Since Pennsylvania law permits it, the lender may elect to pursue the seller for the remaining balance after the deed is transferred. If the seller allows the property to go to foreclosure, in some states like Pennsylvania the lender may have the right to pursue the seller for the remaining balance after the foreclosure sale. A short sale involves a negotiated settlement, whereby the seller and lender reach an agreement on the loss. In most Pennsylvania short sales, the lender will forgive the remaining debt.

---

[1] *The Short Sale Workflow*, published by The National Association of REALTOR®, Spring 2009, pages 5-6.
[2] *California Real Estate Special Report: Legal Guide to Foreclosure-Related Transactions*, 2007.

- *Avoid Bankruptcy.* A mortgage loan is typically the largest debt instrument a person must service. By selling the property via a short sale, a person might avoid bankruptcy altogether. A bankruptcy would affect all of the seller's creditors and be more damaging to the seller's credit rating.

- *Save Money.* Every dollar you spend on a short sale property is a dollar you will not get back. Imagine going to the supermarket, filling up your shopping cart, paying at the checkout counter, *and then leaving the store with no food at all.* Would you do that? Many short sale sellers live in their house for free until the sale, so they save money that would otherwise be paid as monthly rent to someone else had they moved sooner.

TAI TIDBITS...

When you owe someone $5,000 and you're financially struggling, you have a problem. When you owe someone $500,000 and you're financially struggling, *they* have a problem. You'd be surprised how much leverage a person has with their bank when facing foreclosure. The banks do not want to take the property back. There are local, state, and federal assistance programs. When in doubt, pick up the phone and ask for help.

How Lenders Benefit

- *Avoid Excess Inventory.* Banks are in the business of lending money, not owning houses. Many banks are already saddled with far more Real Estate Owned (REO) than they can handle. In many cases, lenders prefer to allow properties to be sold via a short sale.

- *Purge Toxic Loans.* Nonperforming assets hurt a lender's balance sheet. Bank executives face pressure from shareholders to keep the books free from toxic assets. While forgiving some of a defaulted mortgage loan is financially difficult for a bank, the lender then receives a tax write-off that can offset profits.

- *High Costs of Foreclosure.* A June 2007 report from the Joint Economic Committee of Congress stated that the average foreclosure results in $77,935 of costs to the lender, borrower, government, and neighbors. The Joint Economic Committee calculated that the lender will spend $50,000 of that amount on legal fees, court costs, appraisals, maintenance, rehabilitating, insuring, and reselling the property to a third party. Lenders know that taking back properties via foreclosure often results in more losses, so they are willing to permit short sales as a cost-cutting measure. The Joint Economic Committee calculated that the borrower has a typical loss of $7,200 in a foreclosure, to include legal costs, moving expenses, and loss of equity. Neighbors typically suffer a loss of $1,508 due to a decline in area property values. On average, the local government loses $19,227 from a foreclosure.[3]

How Buyers Benefit

- *Bargains.* A patient, opportunistic buyer may be able to purchase a property below fair market value.

- *Equity Creation.* A buyer of a short sale may have purchased a property worth inherently more, thus creating equity that may benefit the buyer now or in the future. Many short sale properties fall into disrepair, and equity can be created by renovating those properties.

- *Sentimental Value.* What is the value of buying the home you really want? The home with the right school district, perfect location, and unique layout? If a buyer really, really has to have a particular house to make their home, then it may be worth the uncertainty and time. How do you place a price on the perfect home?

How Real Estate Agents Benefit

- *More Sales.* Agents who refuse to list distressed properties for sale may cost themselves thousands of dollars in lost commissions. Agents who become short sale experts, or who outsource the processing of a short sale

---

[3] *Sheltering Neighborhoods from the Subprime Foreclosure Storm*, Joint Economic Committee of Congress, April 2007.

to a competent third party, will generate many more listings. In today's market, any sale is a good one.

- *More Homebuyers.* It is a buyer's market, and many buyers specifically are looking for the bargains that may be created by distressed property. Those buyers may bypass certain agents and go to those real estate salespersons who have short sale listings. Also, if an agent helps a grateful borrower sell their property via a short sale, it may only be a matter of time before that person (or their family or friends) calls upon the agent to help them with a new real estate need. The more listings an agent has, the more buyer leads they stand to receive.

- *More Investor Clients.* Real estate investors and landlords are enjoying the bonanza of distressed properties. Investors typically buy (and sell) multiple properties, so an agent with numerous short sale listings may generate many sales with just one client. Some agents prefer to deal with investors and landlords because of their repeat business and quick, unemotional decision-making. Even if an agent refuses to handle short sale listings, that agent will likely represent buyers interested in acquiring properties facing a short sale.

CHAPTER 5. ALTERNATIVES TO A SHORT SALE

Inaction breeds doubt and fear. Action breeds confidence and courage. If you want to conquer fear, do not sit home and think about it. Go out and get busy.

- Dale Carnegie

One national estimate indicates that up to 70 percent of people facing foreclosure do not call anyone for help. They do not call a real estate broker, a lawyer, an accountant, a credit counselor, a third party short sale negotiator, or anyone else who could provide assistance. These property owners are typically embarrassed, fearful, and living in denial. They ignore the problem or believe that there is nothing they can do.

That belief is strengthened because they are often disappointed when they call their mortgage lender to talk about a solution. Many people have reported that their mortgage lender's representatives are completely unhelpful. Distressed homeowners have stated that they are put on hold for over 30 minutes and that their calls are frequently dropped. They have also reported that they are transferred from one clerk to another, and it seems that each lender representative states a different thing. Some lenders assign a "personal representative," but many borrowers have stated that the assigned representative does not return their calls or provide any solutions other than to somehow pay the delinquent amount in full.

After a few frustrating phone calls to the lender, many delinquent borrowers simply give up. They might abandon the house, or they continue to live there for free until shortly before the Sheriff's Sale. Their

TAI TIDBITS...

Once a borrower is delinquent for 90 days on their mortgage loan, the lender has to start the foreclosure process. If you can afford to keep the property long-term, then do not allow yourself to fall behind by more than 90 days. Many delinquent borrowers wait many months before asking for help, and they only limit their options by procrastinating or living in denial.

frustration with the bank creates an adversarial response when the lender calls them. Soon the borrower ignores the lender's calls entirely.

A short sale may have legal, credit, and/or tax consequences. However, a short sale is almost always preferable to a foreclosure for the borrower and the lender.

There are several alternatives to a short sale. These other options include:

1. Make payments to reinstate the loan and keep the property.
2. Sell the property and bring cash to close escrow.
3. Attempt a workout with the lender.
4. Assumption of the mortgage by a buyer.
5. Offer the lender a deed in lieu of foreclosure.
6. Rent the property and move to a more affordable residence.
7. Allow the property to go into foreclosure.
8. Declare bankruptcy.

Make Payments to Reinstate the Loan and Keep the Property

Lenders often will permit a borrower to cure the loan, which means the borrower can make a payment that covers all of the late payments. A homeowner facing default should consider borrowing money from a family member or other lender.

Sell the Property and Bring Cash to Close Escrow

This is known as a make-whole pre-foreclosure sale. The lender does not sustain a loss. The shortfall is paid by the borrower at closing. For example, if a borrower owes $100,000, and the proceeds of the sale generate only $95,000 for the lender, then the borrower can contribute $5,000 at settlement. Alternately, the private mortgage insurer (PMI) may pay the shortfall. In some cases, the hazard insurance company may pay the shortfall if there was damage to the premises covered by the policy.

Attempt a Workout with the Lender

Homeowners are encouraged to work with the lender to forbear the loan, develop a repayment plan, or modify the loan. A forbearance plan is one in which the lender permits a partial payment or a skipped payment if the borrower has an acceptable plan to catch up on the payments. A repayment plan is one in which the lender allows the borrower to pay an additional amount each month until they catch up.

A loan modification is a permanent change to the terms of the note. Loan modification plans include:

- Requiring that property taxes and insurance be included with the monthly payment so the borrower can avoid big bills throughout the year.
- Adding all the missed payments to the loan amount and increasing the monthly payment to cover the bigger loan.
- Switching from an adjustable interest rate to a fixed rate to create stability for the homeowner.
- Lowering the monthly payment by adding years onto the duration of the loan, lowering the interest rate, and/or forgiving some of the loan balance.

TAI TIDBITS...

Many people who attempt a short sale first tried a loan modification yet found out they couldn't qualify, or they defaulted on their loan modification. Your lender won't let you apply for a loan modification and a short sale simultaneously – you must pick one. If you want to keep your home and believe you can still afford it, then try the loan modification. You can negotiate it directly with your lender.

Assumption of the Mortgage by a Buyer

The lender may allow a buyer to assume the mortgage. The lender will determine if the buyer is qualified to handle the monthly debt obligations. Lenders often charge a processing fee to evaluate whether to permit an assumption, and in many cases a new appraisal must be paid for by the buyer and/or original borrower. The lender may require that the original borrower still remain personally liable for the loan should the buyer default on the payments.

Offer the Lender a Deed in Lieu of Foreclosure

This is known as a "friendly foreclosure." The homeowner voluntarily conveys clear property title to the lender in exchange for the discharge of the debt. A lender might consider a deed-in-lieu of foreclosure if the following things happen:

- The lender determines that the borrower faces an involuntary hardship that creates a long-term inability to pay.
- The borrower is cooperative by communicating with the lender and allowing complete access to the property for the lender's inspection and appraisal.
- The borrower is delinquent or faces imminent default.
- The lender sees that the homeowner made a good faith effort to sell the property but was unable to do so.
- There are no other liens or encumbrances against the property.

> TAI TIDBITS...
>
> Most lenders will not consider a deed-in-lieu of foreclosure unless you attempted a short sale first. If the house did not sell in a certain period of time, then the lender may consider or propose the deed-in-lieu of foreclosure.

Rent the Property and Move to a More Affordable Residence

Many Americans have become involuntary landlords, as they've been forced to rent their property to generate money to pay the mortgage loan. This is a good move for a borrower if a suitable tenant is found who can afford a reasonable rent. In some cases, the rent will not cover the entire monthly payment, leaving the borrower to pay some money out of pocket to keep the mortgage current. However, this is typically less painful for a homeowner. Ultimately, market rents may increase to an amount whereby the borrower does not have to come out of pocket to make the monthly mortgage payments. Alternately, the real estate market may improve with time, allowing the homeowner to eventually sell the property for more.

Allow the Property to Go into Foreclosure

In this situation, the homeowner either gives up or fails in all other attempts to resolve the situation. The property is sold at a publicly advertised foreclosure sale or transferred to the mortgage lender if there are no sufficient bids. This situation is considered to be the most damaging to a borrower's credit.[4] Some attorneys may advise their homeowner clients to stop paying the mortgage and live for free in the

---

[4] *The Short Sale Workflow*, published by The National Association of REALTOR®, Spring 2009, pages 5-6.

house until the foreclosure sale. This course of action is often the last resort, given that the homeowner has exhausted all other measures to prevent the foreclosure action. By living in the house until the very end, the borrower does not have to pay rent elsewhere. In such cases, the borrower saves the money that they would have paid the lender so they can have enough to rent a home when the time comes. Remember: only an attorney or accountant familiar with bankruptcy and foreclosure situations should advise a client to stop paying their mortgage. There are serious consequences to this course of action for borrowers.

Declare Bankruptcy

A bankruptcy typically does not prevent a foreclosure action, but it will delay it. Only a bankruptcy attorney or accountant familiar with bankruptcy should advise a client to pursue this course of action. Some bankruptcy actions will eliminate the debt but the lien will still remain until the owner attempts to sell the property. At that time, it is possible the lender may expect some money to release the lien.

CHAPTER 6. WHAT IS BANKRUPTCY?

Money is hard to earn and easy to lose. Guard yours with care.

- Brian Tracy

Bankruptcy is the financial inability to pay one's debts when they are due. Bankruptcy is a federal court procedure for individuals who are unable to pay their debts to settle those debts under a judge's supervision. Bankruptcy is not the same as insolvency. The filing of a bankruptcy case *temporarily* stops foreclosure proceedings.

There are essentially two types of bankruptcy filings for individuals: Chapter 7 and Chapter 13.

Chapter 13 Bankruptcy allows for debt reorganization. The debtor has enough disposable income to submit a reasonable debt payment plan to the court. The plan describes how the creditors will be repaid over a three to five year period. During Chapter 13 Bankruptcy, the creditors are not allowed to collect on the debtor's previously incurred debt except via the court. In general, the person is permitted to keep their property and the creditors end up with less money than the full balance of what is owed.

Chapter 7 Bankruptcy allows for a debtor to keep certain exempt property. Some liens, including mortgages, survive the bankruptcy. Other assets are sold to pay the creditors. If the mortgage lender's

TAI TIDBITS...

The first lawyer I ever consulted told me, "Tai, never ask a lawyer if you need a lawyer because the answer will always be 'yes.'" By all means, consult an attorney. However, if your bankruptcy attorney recommends a bankruptcy, bring your accountant, real estate agent, and any other advocates into the conversation. I've seen several instances where the parties strategized together and recommended that the short sale be conducted first, with a bankruptcy to be declared afterwards.

interests are not adequately protected, the court may allow the foreclosure proceedings to continue.

A bankruptcy will not stop a foreclosure action; it will only delay it. When a person declares bankruptcy, their mortgage lender (as well as other creditors) must stop collection activities for the moment. If a house is worth less than the total mortgage balance, the bankruptcy trustee assigned to oversee the distribution of assets will eventually realize that there is no equity in the property. In many cases, they will release the real estate from the bankruptcy, and at that time the mortgage lender can continue with a foreclosure action.

A homeowner who is seriously delinquent on their mortgage could declare bankruptcy shortly before the foreclosure action to essentially buy more time in the home. Declaring bankruptcy may be a good course of action for someone who has multiple delinquent debts and insufficient income to cover all those obligations. A person considering this should definitely speak with a bankruptcy attorney and their tax advisor.

TAI TIDBITS...

Bankruptcy can be a wise option if you have massive debt and no way to pay all those creditors. However, if the majority of your debt is comprised of your mortgage loan, then it makes sense to go forward with a short sale. A successful short sale should eliminate your mortgage debt. If your income is sufficient to then deal with your other creditors, you will have avoided bankruptcy altogether.

CHAPTER 7. WHAT GOVERNMENT PROGRAMS ARE AVAILABLE?

When trouble comes, focus on God's ability to care for you.

- Charles Stanley

Home Affordable Modification Program

The Home Affordable Modification Program (HAMP) was a federal program designed to help homeowners avoid foreclosure by modifying loans to an affordable and sustainable amount. The program provides loan modification guidelines for the mortgage industry to use. The program stopped taking new applications on January 1, 2017.

TAI TIDBITS...

Need mortgage help? Call the federal government's Homeowner's HOPE™ Hotline at 888-995-HOPE (4673) or go to www.MakingHomeAffordable.gov.

Home Affordable Foreclosure Alternatives

In 2009, the Treasury Department, working in conjunction with the Department of Housing and Urban Development (HUD), introduced the Home Affordable Foreclosure Alternatives (HAFA) program to provide additional options for borrowers who are unable to keep their homes through the HAMP program. HAFA took effect on April 5, 2010 and the program ended on December 31, 2016. For people who were accepted into the program in December 2016, they had to sell their property by September 30, 2017.

FHA Preforeclosure Sale Program

FHA provides mortgage insurance on loans made by FHA-approved lenders. FHA is the largest mortgage insurer in the world. FHA became part of the Department of Housing and Urban Development (HUD) in 1965.

FHA has a Standard Preforeclosure (PFS) program (only for owner occupants) and two Streamline PFS programs (one for owner-occupied properties and the other for non-owner occupied ones). In the Standard PFS program, the seller may have to contribute some of their cash reserves at the time of the sale to help make up the loss.

Below are the eligibility rules and criteria for the Standard PFS program:

- Only for owner-occupants of the house.
- The seller could be current on their mortgage or less than 30 days late on the payments.
- The seller must demonstrate they are at risk of imminent default due to one or more of the following hardships:
    - A loss or reduction in income that was paying for the mortgage loan,
    - A change in household financial circumstances,
    - Death of a co-borrower on the mortgage,
    - Long term or permanent illness or disability of a borrower or a dependent family member,
    - Divorce or legal separation of a borrower, and/or
    - Employment relocation to a job more than 50 miles away.
- First, the lender (also known as the mortgagee) will determine whether the borrower (also known as the seller or mortgagor) is experiencing a hardship by using a Deficit Income Test (DIT). The DIT is calculated by subtracting total monthly expenses from total monthly net income. The DIT is used to determine if a borrower is able to keep paying the mortgage loan. If the borrower's expenses exceed their income each month, then FHA would consider them for a Standard PFS short sale.
- The borrower may have to contribute some of their cash reserves, if any, at the time of the sale. Cash reserves include all non-retirement liquid assets. Prior to being approved for a Standard PFS transaction, the lender must calculate and disclose to the borrower how much that would be. To determine the potential amount, the lender must obtain from the seller:
    - The three most recent monthly bank statements, and
    - The three most recent monthly brokerage statements, and
    - The most recent federal tax return.
- The lender will calculate the total cash reserves using the highest ending balance of each cash reserve asset listed above. A seller with cash reserves greater than $5,000 will be required to contribute, at the time of a short sale closing, 20 percent of the total amount exceeding $5,000 (not to

exceed the difference between the unpaid principal balance and the appraised value of the property) towards the principal balance of the mortgage. If the cash reserve calculation returns a negative result, the seller does not have to contribute anything.

Below are the eligibility rules and criteria for a Streamline PFS program with a non-owner occupant:

- The seller is delinquent 90 days or more as of the date of the lender's review, and
- Each borrower has a credit score of 620 or below.
- The property is not condemned.

Below are the eligibility rules and criteria for a Streamline PFS program with an owner-occupant:

- The seller is delinquent 90 days or more as of the date of the lender's review.
- The property is not condemned.
- Each borrower has a credit score of 620 or below, and
- One or more of the following conditions have also been met:
  - The borrower defaulted on a Trial Payment Plan (loan modification) within the past six months
  - The borrower defaulted on an FHA-HAMP or standard loan modification in the past two years
  - The borrower has been deemed ineligible for a permanent home retention option (Standard Modification, FHA-HAMP, or Formal Forbearance) or Special Forbearance
  - The borrower received a Special Forbearance but did not otherwise qualify for a home-retention option by the end of the forbearance period
  - The borrower was eligible for and offered a home retention option but has a credit score below 580 and chooses in writing to not accept the home retention option.

An owner-occupant short sale seller may receive up to $3,000 at the closing for relocation assistance. They could allocate some or all of that money to cover the buyer's closing expenses and/or junior liens.

TAI TIDBITS...

In the majority of short sales, the seller receives no money. Do not expect your lender to give you money. After all, they are taking a huge loss. If you are fortunate to receive a seller incentive from the lender, consider yourself lucky.

If the property is approved for the PFS Program, an Approval to Participate (ATP) is issued. The date of the form becomes the starting date of the PFS participation. The ATP is a short sale pre-approval. It will state the date by which a signed sales contract must be obtained and the minimum acceptable sale price. The ATP states that the property must be listed with a real estate agent for at least the minimum acceptable sale price. The ATP is valid for four months and can be automatically extended for two months if there is an accepted Agreement of Sale with a buyer. The lender has to delay the foreclosure proceeding during that period.

Once the ATP is issued, one can predict the acceptable sale price if it is below the amount stated in the ATP. HUD adheres to the following Tiered Net Sales Proceeds guidelines:

- For the first 30 days of marketing, lenders may only approve offers that will result in a minimum net sales proceeds of 88 percent of the As-Is appraised value.
- For the next 30 days of marketing, lenders may only approve offers that will result in a minimum net sales proceeds of 86 percent of the As-Is appraised value.
- For the duration of the PFS marketing period, lenders may only approve offers that will result in minimum net sales proceeds of 84 percent of the As-Is value.

For example, let's say that FHA issues an ATP with a pre-approved sale price of $100,000, which would have been the As-Is appraisal value. The minimum acceptable net proceeds for an offer accepted in month 1 of the marketing period would be $88,000. That does not mean the sale price can be $88,000. That means that after real estate commission, realty transfer tax, and closing costs are paid, then FHA must receive at least $88,000. So, assuming that commission, taxes, and closing costs add up to $9,000, the sale price could be $97,000. If an Agreement of Sale were signed in month 3 of the marketing period, then the minimum acceptable net proceeds would be $84,000. Therefore, a buyer could purchase the property for a little less money than earlier in the marketing period.

Sometimes the As-Is appraisal value is well above what buyers are willing to offer. FHA has the following appraisal dispute guidelines (which are not published publicly by HUD but I learned from experience):

- FHA must be provided with three to four comparable sales that sold in the six-month period prior to the date that the appraisal was completed.
- The comparables must be full, Agent Detail Multiple Listing Service (MLS) sheets showing the sold date, sold price, and property description.
- Sales used in the original appraisal cannot be submitted as dispute comparables.
- The comparables must be submitted via email, not via fax or regular mail.
- The seller needs to be advised that the dispute decision is final.
- If the approval is granted to order a second appraisal, the As-Is FMV is final, even if it is higher or unchanged.

There is a serious flaw in the FHA appraisal dispute process. They do not take into account a declining market or a deteriorating house. FHA demands the dispute comparables be ones that sold in the six-month period prior to their appraisal. However, if the property has been on the market for multiple months, those comparables are too old and no longer indicative of the market condition. Furthermore, the house could be losing value due to deferred maintenance, and FHA does not properly account for property deterioration. Therefore, it is critical for the seller or listing agent to liaison with the appraiser ahead of time so the appraiser is made aware of the market conditions.

Fannie Mae and Freddie Mac

Fannie Mae (Federal National Mortgage Association) and Freddie Mac (Federal Home Loan Mortgage Corporation) make loans and loan guarantees. Both are regulated by the Federal Housing Finance Agency (FHFA), which acts as a conservatorship. Fannie Mae and Freddie Mac both permit short sales.

On November 1, 2012, Fannie Mae and Freddie Mac implemented a consolidated, more streamlined short sale approach known as the Standard Short Sale / HAFA II.

These new guidelines allow homeowners with Fannie or Freddie mortgages and who have a documented hardship to pursue a short sale even if they are current on their mortgage payments.

If someone is current on their mortgage, they must be occupying the house as their principal residence. If someone is using the property as a vacation home or investment property, they must be behind on their payments by more than 30 days to be eligible for the program. The property can be vacant but cannot be condemned.

The borrower's total monthly debt ratio, which is the ratio of the borrower's current monthly qualifying expenses divided by the borrower's current monthly qualifying income, must be greater than 55 percent. Military personnel are exempt from the 55 percent requirement. Servicers of will be able to quickly qualify distressed borrowers without waiting for approval from Fannie or Freddie.

The Standard Short Sale / HAFA II program promises a faster process for those who are behind on their payments. Fannie and Freddie will allow up to $6,000 to be paid to a secondary lien holder. The subordinate lien holders must agree to release the borrower from any further debt obligation if they are receiving money from the settlement.

The program calls for servicers to review and respond to a signed buyer offer within 30 days of receiving them. The servicers must provide weekly status updates to the borrower if the offer is still under review after 30 days. The servicers must make and communicate the final decision to the borrower within 60 days of receipt of the offer and a complete borrower response package. Note that even though an offer may have been submitted, the servicer is not obligated to respond within the 30-60 day timeframe if they claim that the homeowner did not submit a complete borrower response package. It is crucial for a borrower to ensure that all the requested paperwork is submitted in a timely fashion.

Fannie and Freddie will waive the right to pursue a deficiency judgment in exchange for a financial contribution when a borrower has sufficient income or assets to make a cash contribution or sign a promissory note. Someone could be asked to make a cash contribution if their cash reserves, including assets such as savings, money market funds, marketable stocks or bonds (excluding retirement accounts) are greater than $10,000 or six times the monthly mortgage payment including principal, interest, tax, and insurance (PITI). If the servicer determines that the borrower has the capacity to make a cash contribution, the servicer must initially request a contribution of 20 percent of the liquid reserves, not to exceed the deficiency. If a borrower who is more than 30 days delinquent is unwilling or unable to contribute 20 percent of their cash reserve, the servicer could potentially accept less as long as there is a specific circumstance that limited the borrower's ability to make a full contribution.

The servicer must evaluate a borrower for a promissory note if the borrower's future debt-to-income ratio is less than 55 percent. If a borrower is deemed to have the capacity to make a promissory note contribution, the servicer must request a five or 10 year term with a payment the borrower can afford in the future. There will be no interest charged. If the borrower is unwilling or unable to agree to the promissory note payment, a lower amount could be negotiated as long as there is a specific circumstance that limited the borrower's ability.

Military personnel who have Permanent Change of Station (PCS) orders will be automatically eligible for a short sale, even if they are current on their payment. They will not be obligated to contribute funds to cover the shortfall.

If an owner-occupant sells their house, and if they were not asked to make a contribution, they will receive a $3,000 relocation incentive.

The sale must be an arms-length transaction. All parties will be expected to sign an affidavit to attest that it is truly an arms-length sale.

The program also allows a real estate commission equivalent to six percent of the sale price. A real estate agent could agree to take less commission. The servicers are expected to provide list price guidance to the borrower after Fannie or Freddie approves a suggested list price and minimum acceptable net proceeds.

There is a deed restriction which prohibits a resale, or flip, of the property within 90 days after the short sale transaction.

HARP and HARP 2.0

HARP was a federal government program for people who are current on their mortgage payments but were unable to refinance their mortgage. To be eligible, the mortgage must have been owned or guaranteed by Fannie Mae or Freddie Mac. This program ended in 2018. In 2018, Fannie Mae created a High LTV Refinance Option for some borrowers.

Fannie Mae High LTV Refinance Option

This program allows borrowers who are current on their mortgage but whose Loan to Value ratio exceeds the maximum allowed for standard cash-out refinance transactions. Borrowers must benefit from the refinance in at least one of the following ways:

- Reduced monthly principal and interest payment.
- Lower interest rate.
- Shorter amortization term.
- More stable mortgage product, such as moving from and adjustable-rate mortgage to a fixed-rate mortgage.

The note date on the Fannie Mae mortgage being refinanced must be on or after October 1, 2017. The borrower must have gotten the loan at least 15 months before applying for a High LTV Refinance. The borrower cannot have any 30-day delinquencies in the past six months.

Here are the minimum LTV ratios:

Principal Residence (1 unit): 97.01%

Principal Residence (2 units): 85.01%

Principal Residence (3-4 units): 75.01%

Second Home (1 unit): 90.01%

Investment Property (1-4 units): 75.01%

Do Fannie Mae, Freddie Mac, FHA, VA, and USDA Waive Deficiency Judgments for Short Sales?

Fannie Mae and Freddie Mac

Fannie Mae and Freddie Mac, under the Standard Short Sale / HAFA II program, instruct servicers to waive their right to pursue a deficiency judgment against the borrower. Under some circumstances, a borrower may be expected to make a cash contribution at a short sale settlement or sign a no-interest promissory note. If the borrower agrees to the cash contribution or promissory note, the remaining debt will be forgiven.

FHA

The Federal Housing Administration (FHA) insures more mortgage loans than any other entity. FHA waives the lender's right to pursue a deficiency on short sales and on foreclosures where an ATP was issued but the property did not sell. In Mortgagee Letter 2008-43, dated December 24, 2008, it states, "A PFS sale must be an outright sale of the property. If a foreclosure occurs after the mortgagor unsuccessfully participated in the PFS process in good faith, neither the mortgagee nor HUD will pursue the mortgagor for a deficiency judgment."

VA

The Veterans Administration (VA) may reserve the right to pursue a deficiency judgment on some loans, and its right to do so may supercede the laws of some states. In the 1961 case, *United States v. Shimer 376 U.S. 374*, the U.S. Supreme Court ruled that the VA had the right to pursue a Pennsylvania veteran who had defaulted on his loan even after the VA seized the house via a Sheriff's Sale. However, it is common for the VA to forgive the remaining debt in a short sale.

USDA

The U.S. Department of Agriculture may reserve the right to pursue a deficiency judgment. In Chapter 6: Liquidation And Acquisition of HB-2-3550, USDA states, "When sales proceeds will not fully satisfy the debt, CSC (Centralized Servicing Center) will make the determination of whether the borrower will be released from personal liability. This determination is based upon a Debt Settlement Package completed by the borrower and forwarded to CSC for review and approval."

How Do I Know If My Mortgage is Through Fannie Mae, Freddie Mac, or FHA?

If you are considering a short sale, it is important to know if your loan is owned or insured by Fannie Mae, Freddie Mac, or the Federal Housing Administration (FHA). Each entity has a particular short sale process.

To find out if you have a Fannie Mae loan, use their online lookup tool by going to www.knowyouroptions.com/loanlookup.

To find out if you have a Freddie Mac loan, use their online lookup tool by going to https://ww3.freddiemac.com/corporate/.

To find out if you have an FHA loan, first check your monthly loan statement since it might display the type of loan. You could also locate your HUD-1 Settlement Statement or American Land Title Association (ALTA) Settlement Statement from when you purchased the house. At the upper right hand corner of the first page, if you see a 13-digit HUD case number, then that means you have an FHA loan. The Federal Housing Administration is part of the Department of Housing and Urban Development.

I'm a Pennsylvania Homeowner Struggling to Pay My Mortgage, and I've Heard About HEMAP. What Is HEMAP?

The Homeowners' Emergency Mortgage Assistance Program (HEMAP) is a loan program designed to help Pennsylvania homeowners who are financially unable to make their mortgage payments. If a homeowner, through no fault of their own, falls behind on their mortgage payments, then they could potentially receive a loan from HEMAP to become current. When someone is approved for HEMAP, the loan is secured by an additional mortgage against the property.

There are two types of mortgage assistance under HEMAP:

1. Non-continuing mortgage assistance loans. Under this program, the mortgage is brought current to a particular date and the homeowner is responsible for all subsequent payments, plus a monthly payment to HEMAP. In some cases, the homeowner might be expected to pay a contribution toward the delinquent mortgage at the time the HEMAP loan is granted.

2. Continuing mortgage assistance loans. Under this program, the mortgage is brought current and then HEMAP subsidizes the monthly payment. The homeowner has to send their monthly payment to HEMAP, and then HEMAP sends the full monthly payment to the mortgage lender on behalf of the borrower.

All HEMAP loans are 24 to 36 months from the date of the mortgage delinquency, or to a maximum of $60,000, whichever comes first. A person must be behind by at least three months on their mortgage to be eligible for HEMAP assistance. When a residential homeowner is behind on their payments by three months, the lender must send a notice known as an Act 91 or Act 6. The notice provides information about HEMAP.

TAI TIDBITS...

Homeowners who want to know more about HEMAP can call the Pennsylvania Housing Finance Agency at 1-800-342-2397 or they can go to https://www.phfa.org/counseling/hemap.aspx

People who receive HEMAP loans are required to pay up to 40 percent of their net monthly income toward their housing expenses. The minimum monthly payment is $25 per month per mortgage assisted.

In August 2012, the HEMAP program was restarted after being unfunded for many months. Pennsylvania Governor Tom Corbett announced that the state had received $66.5 million as part of a federal settlement with the five largest mortgage lenders in the country. The HEMAP program will receive 90 percent of that money over a period of several years. HEMAP will also receive an additional $6 million in 2012 to help with a backlog of applicants facing foreclosure. With the reinstatement of HEMAP, along came the reinstatement of the Notice of Intention to Foreclose, also known as the Act 91 Notice, which mortgage lenders are required to send prior to initiating a foreclosure action.

HEMAP was started in 1983 to help homeowners avoid foreclosure. It is a unique program unlike anything else in the country, and it is just for Pennsylvania residents. HEMAP, which is administered by the Pennsylvania Housing Finance Agency (PHFA), has provided loans to more than 46,000 families. The program boasts an 85 percent success rate for keeping families in their homes. Homeowners who want to know more about HEMAP can call PHFA at 1-800-342-2397 or they can go to https://www.phfa.org/counseling/hemap.aspx.

I Just Received Something in the Mail Called an Act 91. What Is It?

An Act 91 Notice is simply an official notice that the mortgage on a person's home is in default. This notice specifies that the lender aims to foreclose on the property. This is the first step in the foreclosure process. That, however, does not mean the end of the line for the borrower (also known as the mortgagor).

Other important provisions found on the act are as follows:

> TAI TIDBITS...
>
> If you receive an Act 91 Notice, there is no need to panic. It is time to pick up the phone to ask for help.

If you comply with the provisions of the Homeowner's Emergency Mortgage Assistance Act of 1983 (the "Act"), you may be eligible for emergency mortgage assistance:

1. If your default has been caused by circumstances beyond your control,
2. If you have a reasonable prospect of being able to pay your mortgage payments, and
3. If you meet other eligibility requirements established by PHFA.

Some additional rights specified in the Act are:

- The right to sell the property to obtain money to pay off the mortgage debt or to borrow money from another lending institution to pay off this debt.
- The right to have the default cured by any third party acting on your behalf.
- The right to have the mortgage restored to the same position as if no default had occurred, if you cure the default.
- The right to assert the nonexistence of a default in any foreclosure proceeding or any other lawsuit instituted under the mortgage documents.
- The right to assert any other defense you believe you may have to such action by the lender.
- The right to seek protection under federal bankruptcy laws.

The Act 91 Notice states that the borrower has the right to a face-to-face meeting with a housing counseling agency or the lender. The Pennsylvania Supreme Court ruled in *Beneficial Consumer Discount Company v. Vukman* that a lender may still foreclose on a delinquent borrower even if the Act 91 Notice did not include certain language about a face-to-face meeting with the lender.

If someone receives an Act 91 Notice, they generally have at least six months until a Sheriff's Sale. In most counties, it is much more than six months due to heavy foreclosure volume and delays caused by the borrower or lender.

CHAPTER 8. SO HOW DO I KNOW IF I NEED TO DO A SHORT SALE?

I'm not afraid of storms, for I'm learning how to sail my ship.

- Louisa May Alcott

Know How Much Negative Equity You Really Have

Many homeowners are overly optimistic, even delusional, about how much their property is worth. They do not want to sell unless they can at least break even. This mentality is similar to those who own stocks. People are far more likely to sell a stock at a profit than sell a stock at a loss, instead hoping that it goes up before they sell it. In many cases, they hold the underperforming stock for a very long time, all the while watching it decline in value. Instead, if they sold the underperforming stock and invested the proceeds into a high performance stock, they would likely make more money, faster.

Most upside down homeowners believe that they cannot sell until housing prices return to the level they were at when they bought the house. That belief is misguided, as mortgage lenders are approving short sales at a higher rate than ever before. Some lenders are even approving short sales when the loan is current. Since lenders usually absorb the loss in a short sale when they forgive the remaining debt, a short sale may be a worthy business decision for homeowners who are upside down.

Those who want to get back to a break-even level before considering a sale should find out what their property is really worth, with no fluff or fancy optimism. If the property is worth 25 percent less than what it was when they bought it, they may need about a 25-30 percent increase in housing prices to reach that break-even level.

> **TAI TIDBITS...**
>
> Don't give up! I've seen many people just allow the bank to foreclose because they didn't want to face the problem. In the short term, maybe they received comfort from not having to deal with the bank, but in the long term their credit score and ability to borrow money suffers.

With interest rates at historical lows and housing prices so inexpensive too, it may make sense to sell the current house at a loss or via a short sale. Then one could purchase a home with a low interest mortgage and some built-in equity. When housing prices rebound years from now, one would have positive equity instead of negative equity.

Homeowners who want to hold out until they reach a break-even level should examine how much money and time they are costing themselves while they wait just to break even. For some, it may be well over a decade before they do.

The Bank Won't Stop Calling Me. Should I Talk with Them?

I believe you should communicate with your bank on a periodic basis. If you are behind on your mortgage payment, expect up to four phone calls a day per lender. You will also receive a lot of mail.

It is unwise to completely ignore the bank. If you do not communicate at all with your lender, they will probably put you in the category of the people who refuse to pay. That is the worst category for you, as that means they will move the foreclosure process along as fast as possible.

You do not have to answer the phone every single time the bank calls, but it is good to communicate with your lender at least twice a month. If you are considering a short sale, tell the representative. Ask them to send you the bank's short sale paperwork package.

If you are already attempting to sell your property, then tell the person on the phone about it. Reiterate your hardship each time you talk with your lender. If you are still occupying the property, tell the lender so they do not send someone over to verify occupancy.

TAI TIDBITS...

A short sale manager at J.P. Morgan Chase Bank sat with me on a panel in Philadelphia. He told me that they typically have to contact a delinquent borrower over 240 times before the person will communicate with them. If you want to help your situation, talk to your bank.

Why Should I Try a Short Sale? Why Not Let the Bank Take the House?

1. **Foreclosure is a permanent stain.** On all future mortgage applications and on many job applications, people will have to disclose that they lost a property in a Sheriff's Sale. This means that you will likely pay higher interest rates, which can add up to tens of thousands of dollars. This is a credit item that is asked specifically in all credit inquiries. There is no seven-year time limit on this item.

2. **Possible deficiency judgment.** Your bank can still sue you after a Sheriff's Sale and collect any amount they did not recover. In Pennsylvania, the lender has up to six months after the foreclosure sale to initiate the lawsuit, and then they have up to 20 years to collect on a deficiency judgment.

3. **Badly damaged credit.** Credit scores can be lowered by 300+ points per foreclosed loan. Along with bankruptcy, a foreclosure is one of the most devastating credit issues you can have. A short sale has a lesser impact on your credit, and you could be back to normal within two to three years.

4. **Tax liability.** The tax liability in a foreclosure or deed-in-lieu of foreclosure may be higher than in a properly negotiated short sale.

5. **Ineligibility for a government insured loan.** A person who was foreclosed upon will be ineligible for a government insured loan for five to seven years, whereas in a short sale the time period is only two to three years. A foreclosure is the one credit report item that is almost impossible to have repaired.

6. **Potentially damaging for employment.** Many current employers run credit checks. Future employers often do. A foreclosure can put a current position in jeopardy and prevent you from being hired to a good job in the future.

7. **Negative on security clearances.** Security clearances and sensitive government positions, including but not limited to military and law enforcement, can be jeopardized by a foreclosure. Revocation of a security clearance could trigger a job reassignment or a firing.

8. **You have alternatives.** Options include a loan modification, forbearance plan, short sale, deed-in-lieu of foreclosure, government assistance, and renting the home. Contact us at www.shortsalebook.com to learn more.

9. **Do everything you can.** While it may not seem like it now, there will come a time when your current financial troubles will pass. You will feel much better knowing that you did everything in your power to avoid this devastating financial consequence that millions of people face today.

CHAPTER 9. WHAT ARE THE STAGES OF A SHORT SALE?

Bad times have scientific value. These are occasions a good learner would not miss.

- Ralph Waldo Emerson

While many short sales are different, there are three basic stages to each short sale. They are the Document Collection Phase, the Negotiation Phase, and the Closing Phase.

Document Collection Phase

In this stage, the lender or servicer evaluates whether to consider a borrower for a short sale. The lender requests a litany of documents, which typically include the last two federal tax returns, the last two months' bank statements, the last two pay stubs, a financial worksheet detailing monthly income and expenses, a copy of the listing contract showing that the property is for sale, a preliminary HUD-1 Settlement Statement showing the projected amount of money the lender will receive, and an Agreement of Sale with a buyer.

> TAI TIDBITS...
>
> Don't sabotage your own short sale! Be neat and complete with your paperwork. The bank won't proceed with the short sale if they are waiting on a document. So send them everything they ask for, when they ask for it.

This is often the longest stage of a short sale. If the borrower does not submit documents in a timely fashion, then the lender will want all new documents. For example, the lender wants the last two pay stubs. If the borrower submits the pay stubs from February, but waits until April to submit their most recent tax return, then the lender will expect to see the April pay stubs even though the February pay stubs were submitted. Some borrowers have expressed consternation when the lender repeatedly asks for documents that were submitted earlier. Our advice is to keep giving the lender the documents they request. Remember that the lender will not advance the file out of the Document Collection Phase until they are satisfied that they have a complete, up-to-date package.

Negotiation Phase

In this stage, the lender assigns a negotiator. The lender's negotiator may ask for additional documents from the borrower or their representative, who could be a real estate agent, a third party short sale negotiator, or an attorney. If there is a mortgage insurance policy in place, the bank negotiator will communicate with the mortgage insurer to see how much the insurer will pay the lender and if there are any restrictions on how much of a loss can be incurred. The lender's negotiator will liaison with the borrower and their representative. The bank negotiator will likely order an appraisal or Broker's Price Opinion (BPO) to ascertain the current value of the property.

If the bank's requirements have been met, the negotiator will send the short sale package to the decision-maker, who is referred to as "the investor." The investor is a person with approval authority working for the true lender of the money. The investor may take days or even a few weeks to make a decision. That decision will be either be a short sale approval, a counteroffer, or a rejection. The decision is relayed to the bank negotiator, who then informs the seller or their representative.

The short sale approval may include terms or conditions that the seller cannot accept. For example, the buyer might state in the Agreement of Sale that they need a $10,000 credit from the seller for buyer closing costs. The lender may approve the sale price but only allow $3,000 in seller assist for the buyer. If that is the case, then the buyer has to determine if they wish to buy the property and come out of pocket with $7,000 more than they had hoped. It is plausible that a short sale approval could include conditions that the seller or buyer cannot accept.

If there is a counteroffer, the lender will impose a deadline for a response. In some cases, the deadline may be less than 24 hours. In many cases, the deadline might be two or three days away. In some cases, the lender will dictate that the counteroffer is a take-it-or-leave-it amount. In other cases, the lender will be open to a counteroffer from the buyer or seller. In most short sale counteroffers from the lender, the bank calls for a higher sale price. It is important for the seller and buyer to respond to the lender within their time frame, or the bank could close the file.

Once the seller is satisfied with the terms of the short sale approval letter, the short sale advances to the Closing Phase.

Closing Phase

The final stage of the short sale is usually the shortest one. The buyer and seller must make the necessary arrangements for the sale of the property. They must comply with the terms and conditions of the short sale approval letter. If the lender states that the settlement must happen within 30 days, then that is a strict rule. A buyer should not be lackadaisical and believe that they can simply request an extension for more time.

The title agent or attorney must ensure that the closing costs and fees on the final HUD-1 or ALTA Settlement Statement match the approved settlement expenses in the short sale approval letter. The lender only approves certain closing costs, and if there is a discrepancy the lender can unwind the entire sale. We have seen a couple of instances where the lender wired the money back to the title agent because the final Settlement Statement had unapproved closing costs.

Since the lender may have strict rules on which closing costs are approved, in numerous short sales there are still expenses that must be paid at settlement but will not be allowed to be paid out of the proceeds of the sale. For example, assume that a house is located in a development where the Home Owner's Association (HOA) has a transfer fee of $750 that traditionally is paid by the seller of a property. The lender might not approve payment of the $750 fee. However, the fee still has to be paid at settlement. Therefore, the buyer might expect the seller to pay for all or at least some of it. If the seller does not have sufficient funds to pay that amount, then someone else will have to contribute. That could be the buyer, and it could include contributions from the real estate agents, attorneys, and title agent.

In the below example, the seller's mortgage lender approves the sale price of $245,000, the 6% agent commission, the 1% transfer tax, $4,550 in closing costs, and a minimum net proceeds of $223,300. However, just three days before the settlement the title agency discovers that the HOA requires a transfer fee of $750.00. While the parties hope that the lender will generously absorb the additional $750 in closing costs, the lender adamantly refuses to permit some of their proceeds to be used to pay the HOA fee. Therefore, the parties look to the seller to pay the $750, as that is a fee typically paid by the seller in a traditional, non-distressed transaction.

Below are the numbers:

	$245,000	Sale price
-	$ 14,700	6% real estate agent commission
-	$ 2,450	1% Pennsylvania realty transfer tax
-	$ 4,550	Approved closing costs and pro-rated property taxes
-	$ 750	HOA transfer fee not approved by lender
-	$223,300	Mortgage payoff, as the lender takes a $56,700 loss
	$ (750)	Amount that the seller or other parties must pay

If the seller has the $750 and is willing to pay that amount at settlement, then no one else in the transaction has to contribute money. However, in some cases the seller is so short on money that they state that they are unable to pay anything. Then a last-minute negotiation occurs between the buyer, listing agent, and buyer's agent. In some cases, the buyer may pay some or all of the fee as a buyer's assist to the seller's closing costs. Or perhaps the agents will each take a little less in commission.

It is common in short sales for the final numbers to be slightly off from the approved costs mentioned in the short sale approval letter from the lender, which was probably issued a few weeks prior to the settlement. We encourage the seller to save up at least $1,000 just to plan for last-minute expenses. Also, the buyer, agents, and any other participants in the short sale should be open to the possibility that there might be some last-minute contributions required to make the sale happen.

CHAPTER 10. WHAT ARE THE TAX AND CREDIT CONSEQUENCES TO A SHORT SALE?

When we least expect it, life sets us a challenge to test our courage and willingness to change; at such a moment, there is no point in pretending that nothing has happened or in saying that we are not yet ready. The challenge will not wait. Life does not look back.

- Paulo Coelho

Will I Have to Pay Income Tax on My Forgiven Debt?

Here's some background: Unless there is an exemption, the Internal Revenue Service has historically treated forgiven debt as taxable income. That means that people with forgiven debt (such as from a mortgage, credit card, or installment loan) would pay tax as if the forgiven amount were ordinary income.

To give homeowners some relief, President George W. Bush signed the Mortgage Forgiveness Debt Relief Act (MFDRA) of 2007 into law, allowing short sale sellers of their principal residence to pay no income tax as long as they submitted IRS Form 982 with their federal tax return. President Barack Obama and then President Donald Trump signed a few extensions to the MFDRA. Short sale sellers can exclude debt forgiven on their primary residence as long as it was sold between January 1, 2007 and December 31, 2017. Representative Ron Kind of Wisconsin introduced a bill in March 2019 to extend the tax forgiveness through the end of 2019.

Up to $2 million of forgiven debt is eligible for this exclusion ($1 million if married filing separately). Details are on Internal Revenue Service (IRS) Form 982 and its instructions, available on www.irs.gov. Debt reduced through mortgage restructuring, as well as mortgage debt forgiven in connection with a foreclosure, may qualify for this relief. In most cases, eligible homeowners only need to fill out a few lines on IRS Form 982 (specifically, lines 1e, 2 and 10b).

The debt must have been used to buy, build, or substantially improve the taxpayer's principal residence and must have been secured by that residence. Debt used to refinance qualifying debt is also eligible for the exclusion, but only up to the amount of the old mortgage principal, just before the refinancing. **Debt forgiven on**

50

second homes, rental property, business property, credit cards or car loans does not qualify for this tax-relief provision. In some cases, however, other kinds of tax relief, based on insolvency, for example, may be available.

The IRS has historically defined a principal residence as a place where the taxpayer has lived for at least two consecutive years in the last five years. So, it is possible for someone to have moved out recently and still claim a house as their principal residence. Obviously, that means that one cannot claim their new home as their principal residence in the same tax year. The HAFA program states that the borrower can claim a house as their primary residence if they lived there in the past year. Proof of residence can be substantiated by showing utility bills mailed to the house with the homeowner's name on them.

Zillow.com reported in May 2018 that the negative equity rate in the United States was at 9.1 percent in the fourth quarter of 2017. About 4.4 million homeowners owed more on their mortgage than what the house is worth, which was down from the peak of 16 million homeowners in the first quarter of 2012. About 713,000 homeowners owed more than twice as much as their house is worth.

What Can I Do If I Don't Qualify for the Mortgage Forgiveness Debt Relief Act?

So, what can a person do to avoid being hit with higher taxes after a short sale if the Mortgage Forgiveness Debt Relief Act does not apply to them?

Thankfully, there is another way to avoid tax on debt forgiveness that applies to many short sale sellers. Forgiven debts do not need to be counted as taxable income if the debt was canceled in a bankruptcy case, or if the person is insolvent, or if the forgiven debt was intended as a gift. Certain business or farm property may also qualify.

If they do not qualify for the MFDRA, the most relevant option for short sale sellers is the insolvency exemption. It applies not just to principal residences but in some cases to those with forgiven debt from investment properties and vacation homes.

To be considered insolvent, the person's liabilities must exceed the fair market value of their assets. The IRS code states, "A taxpayer is insolvent when his or her total liabilities exceed his or her total assets. The forgiven debt may be excluded as income under the 'insolvency' exclusion. Normally a taxpayer is not required to include forgiven debts in income to the extent that the taxpayer is insolvent. The forgiven debt may also qualify for exclusion if the debt was discharged in a Title 11 bankruptcy proceeding or if the debt is qualified farm indebtedness or qualified real property business indebtedness. If you believe you qualify for any of these exceptions, see the instructions for Form 982." Form 982 is included in the appendix of this book.

If the seller's debts and liabilities exceed their assets by more than the amount of debt forgiven, then they do not have to pay income tax on the forgiven amount. Below is an example:

Susanna's home is worth $200,000, but her mortgage debt is $300,000. When the house is sold for $200,000, Susanna's lender receives $175,000 and they forgive the remaining $125,000.

$200,000	Sale price.
- $25,000	Real estate commission and closing costs.
$175,000	Amount Susanna's bank receives on the $300,000 balance.
$125,000	Amount of debt the bank forgives. Susanna receives a 1099-C.

At first, Susanna panics because she fears that her income will increase by $125,000, thereby pushing her into a 33% tax bracket and increasing her tax bill by over $41,000. However, Susanna's accountant performs some calculations to see if she qualifies for the insolvency exemption:

$225,000	Assets ($200,000 house plus $10,000 savings and a $15,000 car)
- $350,000	Liabilities ($300,000 mortgage plus $50,000 in credit card debt)
$125,000	Insolvency amount

Susanna's accountant states that the insolvency of $125,000 and the 1099-C of $125,000 are a wash. They cancel each other out. Therefore, Susanna does not owe any tax on the canceled debt.

Let's imagine that Susanna had an insolvency amount of $100,000 instead of $125,000. Then she would have to pay income tax on the remaining $25,000 of forgiven debt.

This chapter is not intended as tax advice. I suggest you consult with your tax advisor prior to your short sale and then after the sale. Your tax advisor can examine your particular situation and guide you appropriately.

I Have an IRS Lien. Can I Still Do a Short Sale of My House?

It is possible to sell a house via a short sale even with a federal or state tax lien. In some cases, if the lien is a small amount, the mortgage lender might allow it to be paid in full out of the proceeds of the sale. For example, if the amount of the tax lien is $3,000.00 or less, many lenders will allow it to be paid at the settlement.

If the lien is substantial, the mortgage lender might only permit some of it to be paid. For example, if someone has a $20,000.00 tax lien, their lender might only allow $3,000.00 to be allocated toward the lien. In some cases, the lender will not allow any money to be disbursed to pay off the tax lien.

If the lender refuses to allow any proceeds to be paid toward the tax lien, then it is possible for the lien holder to permit the sale to occur. In other words, it is possible for the IRS or the State Department of Revenue to allow a short sale to occur without any payment toward the tax lien. Such relief is granted on a case-by-case basis, and typically an attorney needs to assist with the negotiation.

To release an IRS lien from a short sale property, the seller may apply for a Conditional Commitment to Discharge Certain Property from Federal Tax Lien. This falls under the provisions of section 6325(b)(2)(B) of the Internal Revenue Code.

To release a state tax lien from a short sale property, the seller may apply for a Personal Income Tax Lien Release from the Pennsylvania Department of Revenue.

CHAPTER 11. IS IT HARDER TO DO A SHORT SALE IF I HAVE MORE THAN ONE MORTGAGE LOAN?

Worry is interest paid on trouble before it comes due.

- William Ralph Inge

In many cases, it can involve more work to successfully negotiate a short sale if there are multiple lienholders. However, not all short sales involving multiple lienholders are difficult.

There are multiple factors to a short sale. Some lenders are more challenging to negotiate with than others. It may be much harder to negotiate a short sale with just one lienholder if that lender is disorganized, unreasonable, bureaucratic, or overwhelmed. If there are multiple cooperative lienholders, a short sale may be easier to pull off than if there is one, difficult lienholder.

There are other critical factors that affect a short sale. One is the seller's willingness to cooperate. Lenders often ask for updated paperwork. A seller who is organized and responsive makes it more likely to obtain a short sale approval than a seller who is slow to submit paperwork. Another factor is the strength of the contract between the buyer and the seller. If a buyer offers a reasonable price and is flexible, that increases the likelihood of the short sale being successful.

TAI TIDBITS...

If there are two mortgage loans, check to see if the proceeds of the sale will be enough to pay off the first mortgage in full. Sometimes you may only have to negotiate with the second mortgage lender. And yes, they are typically willing to take a big loss since they assume they would receive nothing if the house were foreclosed.

The lender's policies factor into the potential for success. If the lender permits a seller assist, that increases the size of the pool of potential buyers. If the lender's staff is not overwhelmed, they can respond more quickly to the parties. As a matter of policy, some secondary lienholders will give in if the first mortgage approves a short sale, so the focus has to be placed on the negotiation with the first mortgage. Some federal short sale programs mandate what the second mortgage can receive, which could make a short sale more likely to be approved by all parties.

The bottom line is that having more than one mortgage does not necessarily make the short sale less likely to be approved. The other factors play a huge role in the outcome.

CHAPTER 12. I WANT TO DO A SHORT SALE AND THE BANK SAYS I NEED TO DISPLAY A HARDSHIP. WHAT COUNTS AS A HARDSHIP?

Fear keeps us focused on the past or worried about the future. If we can acknowledge our fear, we can realize that right now we are okay. Right now, today, we are still alive, and our bodies are working marvelously. Our eyes can still see the beautiful sky. Our ears can still hear the voices of our loved ones.

- Thich Nhat Hanh

A hardship is a situation that renders a borrower unable to continue making monthly mortgage payments and/or unable to sell their property and cover the entire mortgage balance.

Legitimate hardships include:

- The death of a breadwinner.
- Serious illness of a breadwinner.
- Serious illness of a family member, whereby the income earner(s) in a family take time off work to care for the person.
- Serious damage to or a material defect with the property that will not be covered by insurance.
- Loss of a job.
- Failure of one's business.
- Reduced hours at work, which lowers a person's take-home pay.
- Loss of a job by one of the two people in a dual-income household.
- A forced job relocation or new career opportunity, typically more than 50 miles away.
- A divorce, typically one that involves a sharp decline in income and/or significant reduction in liquid assets.
- Increased housing expenses.
- A natural or man-made disaster.

Situations that are not hardships include:

- Desire not to pay, even though the borrower has substantial income or assets.
- Decline in property values (in some areas of the country, like California, Arizona, Florida, and Nevada, the decline is so sharp that it may qualify as a hardship).
- A break-up between a boyfriend and girlfriend who were both on the mortgage.
- A person who has substantial liquid assets and who therefore could easily pay the difference that is owed.
- Depression experienced by the borrower.
- A person who is angry at the bank and wants to stop paying to make a point.

If there is no hardship, then it is unlikely that a short sale may be approved. Check with your lender.

How Does Divorce Affect Foreclosure?

A divorce proceeding generally does not delay a foreclosure action. If someone does not pay their mortgage loan, then the lender's remedy is to initiate a foreclosure action that results in a public auction or the transfer of the property to the bank. Just because there is a divorce action does not relieve the borrowers of the obligation to pay their mortgage.

Mortgage lenders generally consider divorce to be a legitimate hardship when considering a short sale, as divorce can adversely affect the finances of both parties. A mortgage that was easily paid by two income-earners may not be affordable for just one person.

If the divorce decree grants ownership of the house to one person, then it is easy to transfer the deed into that person's name. However, if the divorce decree also stipulates that one party has to be released from the obligation to pay the mortgage loan, there is a possibility that the other party is unable to refinance or pay off the loan. If one party defaults on the loan but both parties remain as borrowers, it is futile to show the mortgage lender the divorce decree. The lender's right to foreclose and report the delinquency to the credit bureaus supersede the divorce decree. In other words, lenders and joint creditors are usually not bound by a divorce decree.

TAI TIDBITS...

If the husband and wife are both borrowers, the lender will not release one party from the obligation to pay even if one spouse removes their name from the deed. Even if a divorce decree was issued long ago giving the property to one party, the credit scores of both parties will be adversely affected should the lender foreclose. I have seen former spouses dragged back together years after the divorce to submit financial paperwork to the lender as part of a short sale negotiation.

CHAPTER 13. NOW THAT I KNOW I NEED TO DO A SHORT SALE, WHAT SHOULD I DO NEXT?

I have learned over the years that when one's mind is made up, this diminishes fear; knowing what must be done does away with fear.

- Rosa Parks

I'm Behind on My Mortgage. Should I Move Out or Stay in the House?

In many cases, it is wise for a homeowner to stay in their house. Many people who are behind on their mortgage payments have an unfounded fear that they will come home one night to find their belongings removed and their door padlocked.

Banks prefer to have someone, particularly the homeowner, stay in the house. Mortgage lenders do not like vacant houses, as they lose value due to break-ins, ice damage in the winter, or lack of upkeep.

A homeowner behind on their payments can save money by staying in their house. Rather than paying for rent somewhere else, they can live rent-free in their house until the property is sold. The money that is saved during this period can be allocated for moving costs, a security deposit, and rent when they eventually move elsewhere.

TAI TIDBITS...

Banks want the property to remain occupied until the property is sold. A vacant or unmaintained property loses value quickly. Vacant properties attract vandals, lose their curb appeal, and may have pipes burst in the winter.

Even if the homeowner is delinquent with their mortgage, they are still the owner of record and therefore remain responsible for the property. The owner could be cited by the local municipality for not maintaining the grounds, such as failure to cut the grass or shovel the snow off the sidewalk. The owner is still responsible for paying property taxes.

The owner is also liable for what occurs on the property. For example, if the owner abandons the property and has a pool, they could be liable if someone falls into the pool even if that person were trespassing. The owner is also expected to maintain insurance on the property. If they cannot afford insurance, they should inform their mortgage lender so the lender can pay for force placed insurance.

Unless there is a compelling reason to move now, such as a job relocation or a contentious divorce, it is wise for a homeowner to stay in the home while the foreclosure process unfolds.

Will My Bank Allow Me to Do a Short Sale If I'm Current on My Mortgage Payments?

Not all short sales involve sellers who are delinquent on their mortgage. Some banks will consider a short sale for a person who is current on their mortgage if there is a legitimate hardship and a documented decline in property values.

Some banks have a policy whereby they will only consider a short sale if the borrower is behind on their payments. This policy can be viewed as absurd, especially if property values have dropped dramatically in the area. On the other hand, why would a creditor want to consider taking less money when someone keeps paying them per their original loan agreement?

A technique used by some people who want to minimize their damage to credit while also having a short sale approved is to deliberately pay their mortgage late, but no more than 29 days late. When a bank receives their mortgage payment 30 or more days late, they inform the credit bureaus. For someone who is looking to borrow money, especially via a mortgage loan, in the next two years, a single instance of being 30 days late can prevent them from obtaining the loan they desire.

A person could choose to not pay their mortgage on time, which after a few days (typically the 6th of the month or later) causes the bank to treat the loan differently than if it were paid on time. The bank may send the file to their loss mitigation department once the loan is delinquent. The bank will call the borrower, and may send letters offering options and assistance. One of the options may be a short sale. Of course, the technique to prevent a 30-day report to the credit bureaus involves the borrower paying their mortgage plus the late fee just before the end of the month. That way the loan never goes 30 days behind, but the bank starts offering options to the borrower. That action may trigger the bank to consider a short sale or loan modification.

60

Some banks unfortunately have the policy whereby the borrower must be at least three months behind before they'll consider a short sale. If that's the case, then the homeowner must make a decision whether they should stop paying the mortgage. In some cases, it may be the best option for a person to stop paying the mortgage. That is a decision that should be made after consulting various professionals and weighing the pros and cons.

The first thing one should do is call their bank to express difficulty in paying the mortgage or selling the house. If asked, many banks will mail a short sale package to the borrower. Some banks will reveal their precise policy on how to qualify for a short sale, while other banks will provide nebulous answers. Sometimes various people at the lender will provide different answers, so it may be worthwhile to keep calling and asking.

TAI TIDBITS...

If you're current on your mortgage, chances are your lender won't consider a short sale. However, if you're late on your payment by more than five days, all of a sudden your bank may be open to various options including a short sale. If you're current on your payments, talk to your lender first. If they won't offer you options, then consider falling behind on your payment by a few days. Your bank might change their tune pretty quickly.

Will I Get Any Money If I Sell My House as a Short Sale?

In the vast majority of short sales, the seller does not receive any money. The bank and other creditors stand to lose thousands of dollars, and so they will not permit the seller to receive any proceeds from the sale. In some cases, the seller is expected to contribute some money at settlement.

There are situations where the seller can receive some money even though it is a short sale. FHA/HUD short sales used to pay $750 to $1,000 as a seller incentive, and now they pay up to $3,000. The federal government's Home Affordable Foreclosure Alternatives (HAFA) program used to pay $3,000 ($10,000 in 2015 and 2016 before the program ended) to the occupant of a property at the time of sale or upon post-settlement move-out.

In 2011, J.P. Morgan Chase and Bank of America rolled out pilot programs known as cooperative short sales. Under the Chase Foreclosure Outreach, Chase offered certain borrowers who were in default up to $25,000 as an incentive to sell. The loan had to be owned by Chase and not merely serviced by them. I saw actual letters sent from Chase offering $3,000, $10,000, $15,000, and $25,000, respectively. Chase told the borrower they would receive the money if they listed with a licensed agent and the contract generated by the agent was acceptable to Chase. The borrower was not expected to submit any financial paperwork. In traditional short sales, the seller constantly submits paperwork displaying their finances. Chase no longer offers as much money as they did in the past. The Chase mortgage relief website can be viewed at https://www.chase.com/mortgage/mortgage-assistance.

TAI TIDBITS...

If you're a short sale seller, do not expect to receive any money. Save up at least $1,000 for closing costs that your bank might not pay. It costs money to sell a property, and you will likely have to pay some of the costs. If your lender does give you a seller incentive to help pay your moving costs, consider yourself lucky.

Bank of America's cooperative short sale program used to offer up to $45,000 to selected borrowers who were in default. I saw one letter where the borrower was told they would receive $23,765.49 upon the sale of their property. The borrower was not expected to submit financial paperwork. In the Bank of America program, the seller and listing agent were told what the list price must be. Bank of America's cooperative short sale program website can be viewed at http://homeloanhelp.bankofamerica.com/en/cooperative-short-sale.html.

It should be noted that the majority of people who sell their property via a short sale will not receive any money. I recommend that sellers save up at least $1,000 in preparation for the settlement. Sometimes the seller will be asked to contribute some money to cover unanticipated closing costs that the bank will not pay.

In some cases, the seller may be expected to pay some money at closing. In most cases where the seller has to contribute something, the amount the seller pays is just to make up the difference on pro-rated taxes, a higher-than-expected water/sewer bill, or some other shortfall that appears at the last minute. For example, if the mortgage lender agrees to take a minimum of $132,655.17 and the closing costs are a little higher than expected, the lender will likely be unwilling to take less than the precise amount they stated. Therefore, the buyer, seller, real estate agents, or other parties must contribute in some way to make up the shortfall. In some cases, the buyer will refuse to pay more, stating that they will not pay for the seller's costs. In such situations, the seller may have to bring some money to closing to cover extra closing costs. Typically that amount would be fairly low, ranging from a few dollars to a couple thousand dollars.

In some short sales, the mortgage lender may stipulate that the seller must contribute some amount of money or the lender may ask the seller to sign a promissory note to pay back some of the remaining debt. The mortgage company must declare any such stipulations in their short sale approval letter, so the seller would know well in advance. In most short sales these days, the mortgage company does not expect the seller to contribute any money as it may be apparent that the seller does not have any funds to give.

Sellers in a short sale should expect to receive no money at closing. If they do qualify for a special short sale program, then they should be grateful to receive what little money they do. The greater financial benefit to the seller is that they will no longer have to maintain a property they cannot afford.

Why Can't I Sell My Short Sale to My Friends or Family? (What Is an Arms-Length Transaction?)

Most banks these days insist upon an arms-length transaction. That is a transaction in which the buyer and seller act independently and have no relationship to each other. They are not related, nor are they business associates. The concept of an arm's length transaction is to ensure that the parties are acting in their own self-interest and are not subject to any pressure from the other party.

If a woman sells a house to her brother, she may sell the house at a discount. If the owner of a business sells his commercial property to an employee, he may sell at a discount or perhaps provide favorable financing.

If two strangers are involved in the sale of a house, it is more likely that the sale price and terms will be close to fair market value. The assumption is that both parties are well informed, well represented, and not under any major duress. The notion is that the seller seeks the highest possible price and the buyer seeks the lowest possible price, and they meet near fair market value.

In a short sale, the mortgage lender insists upon an arms-length transaction to prevent collusion or fraud. There are instances where someone facing foreclosure will ask a family member with a different last name to purchase the house. The lender would forgive the remaining debt, which could be tens of thousands of dollars. The family member who buys the house might then rent or sell it back to the previous owner. That person would have the benefit of continuing to live in the house, but for less money. Furthermore, the lender would bear the brunt of the loss. In addition, the lender assumes that the offer price from the family member might be far below fair market value, further deepening the lender's loss and unjustly enriching the owner.

Most lenders today require that the buyer, seller, and real estate agents sign an affidavit in which they swear that it is an arms-length transaction. Some banks have short sale fraud departments, and they investigate suspicious transactions a few months after they are consummated. If a bank discovers evidence of a non-arms-length transaction when the parties all signed an affidavit to the contrary, the lender can press criminal charges and sue for civil damages. The buyer, seller, real estate agents, and even the title agent or attorney can be sued for committing a fraud. Lenders are losing tens of millions of dollars in fraudulent short sales, and they are serious about finding evidence of illicit activity.

Who is Responsible for Property Maintenance in a Short Sale?

In a short sale, the owner of record is still the owner, and they are responsible for what happens on the premises. Until someone buys the property or the bank forecloses on it, the owner needs to seriously consider maintaining the property.

Some maintenance, such as cutting the grass, helps with the curb appeal while also keeping the owner from racking up fines from the municipality. Keeping the utilities on, even if the house is vacant, can likewise help make the property more appealing to buyers. It is also a good idea to ensure that the house is secured if it is vacant. In winter, it is important for the owner to ensure that they clear ice and snow off the sidewalk. If someone slips and falls, the owner could be held liable. If there is a swimming pool on the premises, the owner needs to ensure that it is secure.

The mortgage lender may have the right to change the locks and secure the house prior to foreclosing on it if they believe that the owner has abandoned the property. The lender may even winterize the house. However, the lender will not cut the grass, shovel the snow, or conduct repairs unless the lender takes ownership via foreclosure.

If the owner lacks the ability to pay for heat in their vacant property in the winter, they should winterize the premises. Alternately, the owner could call the lender to ask if they will winterize the house. The lender often will, and they will add the expense on to the principal balance.

Some municipalities and some judges are placing pressure on mortgage lenders to help maintain properties even before the foreclosure is completed. In a short sale, the lender never takes ownership, so technically they are not responsible for maintenance. However, there is a growing trend across the country where some towns and courts are attempting to compel the mortgage lenders to help cut the grass and secure properties even though they are not the owner. Nevertheless, the owner of record is primarily responsible and should do what they can to keep up certain maintenance to prevent major problems.

If I'm Facing Foreclosure, Can the Bank Change the Locks Before They Foreclose?

When a borrower becomes seriously delinquent on their mortgage, the bank will eventually send someone to the house to verify occupancy and perhaps assess the current market value. If the bank's representative, who may be a real estate agent, contractor, or other third party, deems that the property is abandoned, then the bank may change the locks and secure the premises even if the bank does not yet own it. The bank might even winterize the property to defend against the possibility of water damage from frozen pipes in the winter.

The fine print in most mortgage loan documents allows banks to secure a mortgaged property if their field representative sees that the property is vacant. Even if the doors are locked, the bank may change the locks on an abandoned property. Typically the bank will not tell the owner or listing agent that they've changed the locks. However, the owner and listing agent have the right to request the new keys from the bank. I have seen banks mail the keys or provide a lockbox combination upon request, although sometimes it will take several phone calls to obtain the keys.

If a mortgage lender changes the locks on a vacant house prior to foreclosing on the property, they will not remove any personal items. In other words, the bank should not clean out the house before they foreclose.

If the bank's representative sees that the house is occupied, then they will not change the locks until after a foreclosure sale. A lot of homeowners facing foreclosure have an unfounded fear that the bank will lock them out of their home prior to a foreclosure auction. If the home is occupied, then the mortgage lender will not change the locks, nor will they seize any personal property.

If a person who is behind on their mortgage payments still lives in the property, it is wise for them to inform their bank that the house is occupied. If the bank is notified that someone is living in the premises, then they may not send a field representative to the house.

CHAPTER 14. WHAT IS A STATUS/CONCILIATION CONFERENCE, AND SHOULD I GO?

I think fearless is having fears but jumping anyway.

- Taylor Swift

Some counties across the state schedule what is known as a status conference, or a conciliation conference, to help homeowners who face foreclosure. The status conference is like a timeout in sports. It involves the judge who presides over the lender's foreclosure lawsuit against the borrower.

A brief meeting is scheduled between the borrower and the mortgage lender's attorney with the judge presiding. The judge wants to see if the homeowner is working toward a loan modification, short sale, deed-in-lieu of foreclosure, or other solution to prevent the foreclosure. The judge is also evaluating the borrower to see if they are a deadbeat who probably deserves to lose their house. The judge also wants to see if the mortgage lender's attorney understands the case and is willing to entertain the borrower's proposed solution.

TAI TIDBITS...

If your county gives you an opportunity to meet before a judge, then go! The judge in his or her sole discretion can grant you more time to work out a solution with your lender. If you don't attend, then expect the judge to allow the foreclosure lawsuit to continue unabated.

If the borrower or the lawyer for the bank fails to show up to the status conference, that may annoy the judge. There are instances where the attorney does not show up, and the judge grants an extension in the foreclosure process for the homeowner. If the borrower does not show up, the judge will likely allow the foreclosure suit to continue unabated.

I strongly suggest that the homeowner show up for the status conference if they wish to conduct a short sale, loan modification, or deed-in-lieu of foreclosure. If the borrower does not attend, it is highly likely that the judge will allow the foreclosure to move forward at full speed. The judge has the power to delay the foreclosure action, and the judge wants to help homeowners who are trying to help themselves. Also, there are many instances where the bank's attorney does not attend, so their failure to show up can shift the matter in favor of the homeowner.

If a homeowner is attempting a short sale, they should print out the listing of the house and bring a copy of the Agreement of Sale if the property is under contract. They should also bring their most recent mortgage statement or a letter from the lender about the foreclosure. The homeowner is welcome to bring their attorney if they have one, but a lawyer is not necessary. A status conference typically only lasts a few minutes. If the borrower shows up prepared, they may find that the judge encourages the bank's lawyer to work toward a solution that does not end in foreclosure.

CHAPTER 15. TWENTY WAYS A SHORT SALE CAN BE DELAYED

You gain strength, courage, and confidence by every experience in which you really stop to look fear in the face. You must do the thing which you think you cannot do.

- Eleanor Roosevelt

Short sales are often referred to as "long sales." Ain't that the truth? Many sellers, buyers, and real estate agents find that short sales may take much longer than initially expected.

So what causes delays (or perceived delays) in a short sale?

1. The seller does not submit the paperwork their mortgage lender requires to evaluate the short sale.

2. The mortgage lender's staff is inundated or disorganized.

3. The mortgage lender closes the file and it must be started again from scratch.

4. The listing agent and the seller price the property way too high, so no one makes an offer.

5. The buyer backs out of the transaction.

6. The property loses value from vandalism, theft, frozen pipes, or deferred maintenance, which causes the buyer to walk away or demand a lower price that the lender will not approve.

7. The person or company negotiating the short sale for the seller is disorganized, inexperienced, inundated, or otherwise slow with the processing of the file.

8. The mortgage lender issues a counteroffer that forces the buyer and seller to take time to negotiate.

9. Another lienholder or creditor negotiates as well.

10. The mortgage lender loses the file.

11. The seller is unable or unwilling to pay certain closing costs, which forces the other parties to negotiate how to pay those costs.

12. The appraiser or agent sent by the lender to the property is unable to access the property on the inside.

13. The mortgage lender restructures or institutes new software that the staff takes time to learn.

14. The mortgage lender changes the locks on the property, and the seller or buyer demands access before moving toward settlement.

15. Emotional outbursts among some of the parties force others in the transaction to engage in time-consuming activities to defuse the rash decisions fueled by those emotions.

16. A private mortgage insurer is involved and therefore must also approve the short sale.

17. A government agency or other organization, like Fannie Mae, Freddie Mac, the Department of Housing and Urban Development (HUD), or the Veterans Administration (VA) is involved and therefore must also approve the short sale.

18. A seller or tenant refuses to move out in a timely manner, so the buyer delays the purchase until the house is vacant.

19. A title agent prepares an inaccurate HUD-1 Settlement Statement, which must be revised.

20. The mortgage lender's system has a sole decision maker or influencer, and that person is away from the office at a critical moment.

Some of the Nutty Reasons Why Mortgage Lenders Make Short Sales Take So Long.

In many situations, the mortgage lender or servicer cannot get out of their own way. They create inane reasons why they cannot make a decision on whether to approve a short sale. Below are just some of the reasons I have seen.

1. The sale contract had the buyer's name misspelled in one section, and the servicer refused to make a decision until a fully corrected contract was issued. The contract had the correct spelling of the buyer's name

elsewhere, and the buyer's signature was authentic, but the servicer insisted upon having no misspellings anywhere.

2. The IRS tax return was not signed by the seller, and the lender refused to consider a short sale until the seller signed the tax return. Note that the seller's tax preparer had submitted the tax return to the IRS on the seller's behalf. The IRS considered the tax return to be valid with the tax preparer's signature. However, the lender insisted upon having the seller sign the tax return even though it was good enough for the IRS.

3. The bank negotiator went on a three week vacation, and no one else in the company would cover for him in his absence.

4. The sale contract did not have the seller's middle initial, and the servicer refused to render a decision until the middle initial was added. Even though the contract was legally sufficient in that state, it was not good enough for the servicer.

5. The bank negotiator was fired and no one else at the bank took over the file. It simply sat in limbo for months. One would think that a manager who fired a staff member would reassign the file to someone else, but apparently that did not happen.

6. The bank stated that they would not speak with the seller because the seller was represented by an attorney. The bank stated that even though the seller is the borrower and was being called several times a day as part of the bank's collection efforts, their policy is that when the seller hires an attorney they only speak with the attorney. Here's the kicker: the bank would not speak with the attorney because they could not find the Authorization to Release Information Form in which the seller granted permission for the attorney to speak to the lender. So the bank would not talk to the borrower, who was trying to grant permission for his lawyer to communicate with the lender.

7. When dealing with one bank negotiator at Wells Fargo, her voicemail stated that she would not return any calls. Interestingly enough, her voicemail was full and thus no one could leave any messages either.

8. A Bank of America negotiator stated for weeks that the investor was close to making a final decision. Eventually, the buyer threatened to terminate

the contract. When pressed for an answer, the Bank of America negotiator admitted that he had never submitted the file to the investor for a decision. When told to submit the file immediately or the buyer would walk away, the negotiator replied that the appraisal had expired and therefore he would have to wait for a new appraisal. The buyer walked away, and shortly thereafter thieves stole all the copper and wiring from the house. Bank of America lost tens of thousands of dollars because a file sat on the negotiator's desk.

How Long Does It Take to Do a Short Sale?

The amount of time it takes to sell a property via a short sale depends on a number of factors, all of which must align to produce a sale. It may take anywhere from a couple of months to well over a year to complete a short sale.

Below are some of the factors:

1. **The seller's responsiveness.** One of the biggest causes of a delay in the short sale is the seller themselves. Their mortgage lender asks for documentation throughout the short sale process, and many times the lender will ask for updates on paperwork that was already submitted. Many sellers are slow to produce paperwork, either because they are disorganized, emotionally upset, or confused about the nature of the paperwork. The ideal short sale seller responds immediately to requests for paperwork without questioning why the lender wants it.

2. **The lender's internal policy.** Each lender has its own timeframe for a short sale. They may have a policy on who has authority to advance or escalate the file to the next stage. Many borrowers attempt a loan modification first, and most lenders will not consider a short sale while a loan modification is being considered. In most cases, the lender's staff is overwhelmed and that delays the process.

3. **Involvement of other lienholders.** If there are multiple lienholders, that might prolong the short sale negotiation because everyone has to approve the sale. In most cases, each lienholder may attempt to limit what the other lienholders receive, which can complicate the negotiation.

4. **Involvement of a mortgage insurer.** If a mortgage insurer is involved, then they must agree to the amount of the loss that the lender will take. That injects an additional decision maker into the process. The mortgage insurer may have certain rules about what they would approve, and the lender may have to abide by those guidelines.

5. **Involvement of a Government Service Entity (GSE).** If Fannie Mae, Freddie Mac, the Veterans Administration (VA), the U.S. Department of Agriculture (USDA), or the Federal Housing Administration (FHA) is involved, then they too have to approve the short sale. That injects an additional decision maker into the process, and each entity has their own procedure.

6. **The type of short sale program.** There are federal short sale programs, like the Fannie Mae and Freddie Mac Home Affordable Foreclosure Alternatives II (HAFA II). There are lender programs, like the traditional short sale and the cooperative short sale. Each program has guidelines on timing. One program may require that the property not have

> **TAI TIDBITS...**
>
> I hear this all the time: "Why isn't this short sale approved? It's been going on for eight months."
> Understand that short sales are not linear, nor cumulative, in the passage of time. In other words, the amount of time is irrelevant. What matters is whether a specific set of tasks have been completed in a specific time frame in the eyes of the bank. A lender could close a file that's been open for six months simply because the seller's negotiator did not submit a document in time. Then the process must be restarted. The lesson: When a lender asks for a task to be completed, do it right away.

an offer on it yet, while another lender's program may only consider a short sale if there is a signed contract with a buyer.

7. **Involvement of a third party vendor negotiating for the lender.** Some lenders like to use third party vendors to help negotiate with the seller. These third party vendors work for the bank and may have their own procedures in addition to the lender's rules.

8. **Involvement of a third party vendor or attorney negotiating for the seller.** A third party vendor or attorney working for the seller may have their own guidelines. They may only advance the short sale if all paperwork is received from the seller up front. If the seller fails to submit all the necessary documents, that cripples their ability to negotiate on the seller's behalf.

9. **The ability of the listing agent to procure a buyer.** Even if the short sale approval process is moving along quickly, it is essential to have a ready, willing, and able buyer. Without a buyer, there is no closing. Some properties, such as houses in need of repair, may only appeal to a certain segment of the buyer pool. If a lender pre-approves a short sale at a certain price, but buyers believe that price to be too high, then there will be extreme difficulty in finding a buyer.

10. **Expiration of the appraisal or Broker's Price Opinion (BPO).** Even if there is a buyer and if the process is moving along quickly, a lender may slow the negotiation because the previous valuation of the property is too old. Some lenders may only consider an appraisal if it occurred in the past three months, while others may only approve a short sale if the appraisal is less than six months old. Also, it may take days or weeks for an appraiser or BPO agent to submit their report.

11. **The amount of time it takes to prepare a preliminary ALTA Settlement Statement.** Sometimes a title agent or attorney may not be able to put together the preliminary settlement statement fast enough. A lender needs to see a preliminary ALTA statement prior to making an approval decision. The title clerk may have insufficient information about the outstanding liens and payoffs to meet the deadline posed by the lender. The lender could arbitrarily close a file if a single document is not received.

74

12. **The buyer's willingness to stay in the deal.** Some buyers back out of a short sale even when it is approved. They may lose their ability to obtain financing, or they may find a more enticing property to buy. Some buyers become frustrated and terminate their contract, which may occur mere days before an approval is granted.

CHAPTER 16. WHAT IS THE NORMAL TIME FRAME FOR A SHORT SALE?

It is not in the still calm of life, or the repose of a pacific station, that great characters are formed. The habits of a vigorous mind are formed in contending with difficulties.

- Abigail Adams

In terms of what is normal, each lender has their own policies on when decisions may be rendered. Each lender has its own internal deadlines. Of course, the lenders generally do not abide by their own published time frames and deadlines. Asking if a short sale situation is normal is like asking if a war is normal. One can predict certain things based upon past experience and knowledge of the other parties, but every short sale and every war are different and inherently unpredictable. Lenders frequently do not abide by their own (published or unpublished) deadlines, nor do they hold themselves accountable to their own deadlines.

Successful short sales require a cooperative seller, a patient buyer, a reasonable appraisal by the seller's lender, skilled real estate agents, a good negotiator working for the seller, and a mortgage lender that is willing to communicate frequently with that negotiator. If one party to the short sale is not participating or cooperating, then the entire transaction is in jeopardy.

There are tales of short sales that happen in two months. There are also short sales that take more than two years. Many short sales take four to six months from the date of the listing to the settlement date. A good number of short sales fail.

The parties in a short sale transaction should be flexible and committed. They should focus more on the outcome and less on the process. Their flexibility and commitment may be rewarded in the end.

In a short sale, the buyer and buyer agent should refrain from scheduling a firm closing date until short sale approval is granted for all liens and the seller expresses that they are satisfied with the approval terms. Even though the seller may receive a short sale approval does not mean that they are willing to accept the terms. If an

76

agent or attorney is representing the seller, they should not tell the buyer that there is an approval until after the seller expresses that they are satisfied with it.

If the buyer and buyer agent insist upon scheduling a settlement date, they should establish a cut-off date in advance of the proposed closing date to postpone the closing should they be waiting for the short sale approval(s). For example, if the buyer wishes to pick a settlement date of the 30th of the month, their cut-off date could be seven days in advance. That way, if there is no short sale approval by the 23rd, the buyer can elect to postpone the proposed settlement and move-in date past the 30th. In other words, the buyer should not be taking a day off work, nor packing up the moving truck, nor terminating their lease until there are short sale approvals for all liens that the seller finds to be satisfactory. If a buyer picks an arbitrary closing date, they are setting themselves up for a costly disappointment.

CHAPTER 17. SHOULD I PAY MY MORTGAGE, INSURANCE, AND PROPERTY TAXES?

You may encounter many defeats, but you must not be defeated. In fact, it may be necessary to encounter the defeats, so you can know who you are, what you can rise from, how you can still come out of it.

- Maya Angelou

What Is a Short Sale Going to Cost Me?

First, you should look at a short sale from the standpoint of what it will save you. A short sale can save you from an onerous debt obligation. A short sale can help put you on the path to a better credit score. A short sale can free you from the liability of owning a house that you cannot afford. A short sale will help reduce stress in your life. What is the value of closing a rough chapter of your life and starting fresh on a new chapter?

A short sale does not necessarily have to cost you much money. In the next two chapters, you will see that it may be in your best interests to pay for certain things like homeowner's insurance, the utilities, and some property maintenance. I also suggest you save at least $1,000 in preparation for unexpected settlement expenses.

Pay close attention to the terms of the real estate contract you sign with a buyer. The standard contracts used in Pennsylvania state that the seller must keep the utilities activated for the buyer's inspection and that the seller must maintain the property in its present condition until settlement. Some short sale sellers stop paying for utilities because they want to save money. However, shutting the utilities off prematurely may cause severe damage in the winter, or at the very least it will irk the buyer who expects the utilities to be on for their home inspection. A home inspector cannot verify that the heating system, electrical wiring, and plumbing are functioning properly if the utilities are shut off.

In several short sales I worked on, the sellers shut off the heat in the winter and the water pipes burst everywhere. In one instance the seller's insurance paid to fix the damage, and the lender agree to extend the short sale approval. The buyer had to delay their move, yet in the end it worked out. In another situation, the seller hired contractors to repair their house while expecting the homeowner's insurance to

78

cover the cost. The insurance company ultimately denied the claim when their adjustor discovered that the electricity was shut off by the seller. The contractors sued the seller for the all the work they had performed. On top of all of that, the buyer terminated the contract due to all the problems.

Should I Still Pay My Property Taxes?

In most short sales, the lender will allocate some of the proceeds to pay the property taxes. That includes the delinquent taxes. While the homeowner is technically responsible for the payment of property taxes, they have to make a business decision on whether to pay the taxes. If someone is in financial distress, it is likely they will not have the means to pay the taxes. Many borrowers who are behind on their mortgage payments are also behind on their property tax payments. Every dollar a homeowner spends on a short sale property is a dollar that they will not get back.

If the owner pays the taxes in a short sale, then they will not receive any pro-rated credit refund at the settlement. The lender keeps the credit. If the owner does not pay the taxes, they lender will typically pay the back taxes. In other words, if the owner pays the taxes, all of the money paid ultimately benefits the lender. If the owner does not pay the taxes, the lender may end up covering that amount.

If the property is scheduled for a tax sale, in many cases the lender will pay the taxes. A mortgage lender has to be notified of a scheduled tax sale so they are given the opportunity to act to protect their interests.

Most people who need a short sale choose not to pay the property taxes in the hope that the lender covers that expense. The lender usually does.

Some mortgage companies pay property taxes on behalf of the owner via an escrow account that the owner is supposed to pay into on a monthly basis. If a person is delinquent for only a few months and they have an escrow arrangement with their mortgage lender, there may be enough funds in the escrow account to pay off the current year's taxes. The lender might even temporarily fund the escrow account if there is a slight shortfall. If the borrower believes they can sell the property in the near future or they reach an alternative arrangement with the lender, no other property taxes may be due at that time.

If the borrower is more than a year behind on payments, then any escrow account will probably have no money left. If nothing is done, the property taxes will go unpaid. Eventually a tax sale will be scheduled, with the borrower and the lender being notified of the sale. In many cases, the mortgage lender will pay the delinquent property taxes shortly before the tax sale just to protect their interest in the property.

If a borrower is facing foreclosure, it is a judgment call whether they should pay the property taxes. Assuming they have the funds to pay the property taxes, it is often wise to pay the delinquent taxes if they have equity in the property. That will eliminate the tax sale and buy the owner time to sell the property or find another solution to the foreclosure action. It protects the owner's equity.

If a borrower is attempting to sell their property via a short sale, the property taxes are often paid out of the lender's proceeds at the sale provided that the back taxes were included on the preliminary HUD-1 Settlement Statement submitted to the lender. It may not be as prudent for the owner to pay the property taxes in a short sale, as every dollar they spend on the property is a dollar that they will not recover.

If a mortgaged property is sold at tax sale, the mortgage obligation may still exist. Depending on the type of tax sale, the original borrower will still be on the hook to pay the mortgage loan while the new owner will have the mortgage clouding the property's title. Until that mortgage is paid, the lender can pursue the seller for the balance while continuing with the foreclosure action.

What's the Deal with Property Tax Sales?

If property taxes are not paid, the property could be sold at a tax sale. The Pennsylvania Real Estate Tax Sale Act (RETSA) holds that all lawfully levied taxes on property constitute a first lien on the property. Delinquent taxes can be higher than the mortgage in order of priority.

Each county has a Tax Claim Bureau that collects all the property taxes. The taxes become delinquent in the year following the year in which they were due. The Tax Claim Bureau will send a notice of the delinquent taxes by registered or certified mail with return receipt to the owner's address. If the post office cannot deliver notice, then it is prominently posted on the property.

Upset Tax Sale

The first type of tax sale is the Upset Sale. An auction is held, and the buyer takes the property subject to the claim of all recorded mortgages, liens, ground rent, claims, and tax liens from the Pennsylvania Department of Revenue. To clear the title, the buyer must pay off the amounts outstanding against the property. Some people foolishly bid on property at an Upset Sale, thinking that they can buy the property for just a few thousand dollars. What they do not realize is that there are probably many other liens and claims against the property that must be satisfied before there can be clear title. In many cases, the mortgage lender will pay the back taxes before the Upset Sale to protect their interest.

Judicial Tax Sale

If the Upset Sale cannot produce a bidder who will pay the upset price, the Tax Claim Bureau may petition the county's Court of Common Pleas to permit a Judicial Sale. For instance, a house may have a sizable mortgage against it, causing the bidders at the Upset Sale not to bid high enough to take ownership of the property subject to the mortgage. The Court of Common Pleas can set a sale date. The high bidder at a Judicial Sale takes title to the property free and clear of all mortgages, taxes, and liens. Ground rents still remain. In most cases, the mortgage lender will pay the back taxes to prevent a Judicial Sale.

Right of Redemption

The former owner of a property sold at a tax sale could redeem the property within one year from the date of the acknowledgment of the Sheriff's Deed that awards ownership to the high bidder. To buy back the property, the former owner must pay the amount bid at the tax sale plus other costs and any liens or encumbrances that were paid. There are some exceptions. For instance, if the property were vacant or abandoned by the former owner, then they might not have the right to redeem it.

If I'm Current on My Mortgage Loan, Can I Still Do a Short Sale?

In some situations, certain banks may consider a short sale on a property where the borrower is current with their payments. In a state where foreclosures are rampant, such as Nevada, California, Florida, and Arizona, banks are far more likely to consider a short sale for someone who has not missed a payment. Even so, I have seen multiple cases in Pennsylvania where a short sale was approved for someone who never missed a payment. A person who is current on their mortgage needs to display a legitimate hardship. They typically have to be in danger of imminent default. In other words, they must demonstrate that they're financially struggling to pay all their bills, which indicates that mortgage default is likely.

In some cases, however, banks will only consider a short sale if the borrower is behind on their payments. Some lenders will consider a short sale if a person is more than five days late. Many banks state that the borrower must be at least 30 days behind. Other banks will only consider a short sale if the borrower is delinquent by more than 90 days. The national trend is that more and more banks are permitting short sales for people who are current on their mortgage but likely to default in the near future.

If there is a compelling reason to sell, a verifiable hardship, and it is clear the market value is less than the amount owed, a seller's first step should be to talk to their bank. They should ask their lender about the criteria needed to qualify for a short sale. If the lender states that the borrower must be delinquent by a certain period of time, then the borrower needs to make a business decision on whether to stop paying.

Some people find that they must be delinquent for a short sale to be permitted, but they still want to preserve their good credit rating as much as possible. If a person is 30 days behind on their mortgage, that delinquency is reported to the credit bureaus. For the next two years, lenders will likely shun that person because of the delinquency. Even if the person qualifies for a new loan, the interest rate will typically be higher and more costly over time. Some lenders evaluating a person for a loan will accept one 30-day late payment on one credit line within the past 24 months if there is a written explanation.

A technique some people use is to deliberately fall behind on their mortgage payment. Those who want to avoid going 30 days late if they can help it have the option to pay their mortgage about 25 days late. They will have to pay a late fee along with the monthly payment. This technique flags the loan as delinquent in the lender's system, but the borrower avoids a negative hit to their credit since they were never truly 30 days late. This could spur the lender to offer a short sale to the borrower.

Other people strategically default on their mortgage, whereby they stop paying altogether. After doing the math, they realize that it is pointless to continue paying. They might as well save up the money they would have paid to the bank, and they recognize that they have no equity in the property whatsoever.

Lawyers and accountants can recommend to their clients that they stop paying the mortgage to put into motion the events that will lead to a short sale or deed-in-lieu of foreclosure. A real estate agent should never tell their client to stop paying. A decision to stop paying one's mortgage is a tough one, and a person should evaluate all their options carefully.

Should I Still Pay for Homeowner's Insurance?

If a person owns a house, they are responsible for maintenance and they are liable for what happens on the premises. The cost of paying for insurance coverage is much smaller than the cost of catastrophic loss. It is important to avoid owning a house that is uninsured.

If a house is not insured and it burns to the ground, the owner is still responsible for removal of the debris and payment of the mortgage loan. If someone is injured on the premises and the owner is at fault but does not have insurance coverage, the owner faces a costly challenge.

In wintertime, the owner is responsible for preventing damage from frozen pipes. If the owner is unable or unwilling to pay for heat, then the house should be winterized. If the owner is unable to pay for the cost of winterization, they should notify their mortgage lender immediately. In many cases the mortgage lender will pay to winterize a house add the cost to the principal balance.

> TAI TIDBITS...
>
> If you're debating whether to pay for homeowner's insurance or property taxes and you can't pay both, pay the insurance. Insurance protects you. Besides, your lender will typically pay the delinquent taxes to prevent a tax sale.

If the pipes burst from frozen water, then the insurance company might not pay to repair the property if the adjustor deems that the owner was negligent. I knew of a case where owners facing foreclosure moved out of their house and stopped paying for electricity. The house had electric heat. When the pipes burst from freezing water, the house became flooded in multiple places inside. The owners, believing that their insurance would pay to repair the house, hired contractors to make almost $10,000 in repairs. When the insurance adjustor called the electric provider and found that the owners had shut off the electricity, the insurance company decided not to pay for any repairs due to owner negligence. The contractors then sued the owner for payment.

If a homeowner cannot pay for insurance to cover their house, then they should notify their bank immediately. Many banks will pay for what is known as force placed insurance. That insurance is generally more expensive than insurance that the owner could obtain through a normal provider. The bank will add the cost of the insurance to the principal balance.

If a seller is under contract with a buyer, the seller is responsible for maintaining the property in its present condition until the closing. If the pipes freeze before the sale, the owner will be responsible for repairing the property to the condition it was in before the damage. Without insurance, the seller will be in an expensive situation. If they fail to repair the property for the buyer, the buyer could sue the seller. Therefore, it is imperative that a seller maintain homeowner's insurance on their property.

Will I Go to Jail for Not Paying My Mortgage?

No! A borrower will not go to jail if they default on their mortgage loan, but they could face criminal charges in a couple of extreme situations described below.

In some states like Pennsylvania, foreclosure involves judicial proceedings. In other words, the lender must hire an attorney who initiates a foreclosure lawsuit against the borrower. The lawsuit does not involve any criminal charges against the borrower. It is merely a civil proceeding that involves the lender's attempt to collect a debt or be given ownership of the property in exchange for the unpaid debt obligation.

If a borrower fails to maintain their property prior to being foreclosed, the local municipality could issue a citation and/or a fine. Common citations include failure to keep grass cut, leaving pets behind, having an unfenced or tepid swimming pool, or leaving a house unsecured. Some municipalities will even condemn a property. If the borrower fails to address the issues and pay the fines, some municipalities have the ability to take the borrower to court. In rare cases, failure to show up for court could result in an arrest warrant being issued.

If a borrower deliberately trashes a house, it is possible for the lender to sue them after the sale for destruction of property and perhaps even press criminal charges. While rare, it is done in cases where the borrower creates major damage to the house. I have seen cases of angry borrowers clogging toilets and sinks with concrete mix or stopping the drains with other things like tennis balls. They then turn the water on and leave it on. In other cases, borrowers have ripped out all the fixtures and appliances.

In some blighted cities, lenders have taken the unusual step of not foreclosing since they determine that the property's value is so low that it is better to not take it back. This is known as a bank walkaway, where the bank charges off the loan and stops the foreclosure action. Therefore, the borrower remains as the owner. The city can then issue citations against the owner for failure to maintain their property. In some cases we have seen, the owner walked away from the property only to find out years later that they still owned the property. The city may even have the right to demolish the property and bill the owner for the cost. In rare cases, failure to respond to the city's citations or court hearings could result in an arrest warrant being issued.

CHAPTER 18. IF I VACATE MY HOUSE, WHAT SHOULD I KNOW?

The brick walls are there for a reason. The brick walls are not there to keep us out. The brick walls are there to give us a chance to show how badly we want something. Because the brick walls are there to stop the people who don't want it badly enough. They're there to stop the other people.

- Randy Pausch

Should I Shut Off My Utilities If I Vacate the House?

As the owner, you are still responsible for what happens on and to the premises.

In wintertime, the owner is responsible for preventing damage from frozen pipes. If the owner is unable or unwilling to pay for heat, then the house should be winterized. If the owner is unable to pay for the cost of winterization, they should notify their mortgage lender immediately. In many cases the mortgage lender will pay to winterize a house and add the cost to the principal balance.

If the owner shuts off the utilities, it can cause problems when the buyer conducts their home inspection. Many real estate contracts state that the seller will have the utilities on for inspections. If the buyer has to activate the utilities, they may be reluctant to make an offer in the first place, or they may simply make a lower offer than what they originally intended.

Also, if the electricity is shut off, that can wreak havoc with showings, particularly showings in the evening. If the house is dark, buyers are likely to be less interested in the home. Keeping the electricity on makes showings run much more smoothly.

When the buyer conducts their pre-settlement walk-through inspection of the house, they will feel more comfortable if the utilities are on. If the electricity and water are on, that could prevent any last-minute doubts or late-stage negotiation. If financially feasible, it is wise to keep the utilities on. At the very least, keeping the electricity and the water on can aid in the smooth sale of the property.

Can the Bank Lock Me Out of the House?

If the mortgage lender has not foreclosed on a house and it is still occupied, then the lender is not allowed to change the locks. Many homeowners have an unfounded fear that they will come home one night to find they are locked out and their possessions are seized. Many people move out of their house prematurely due to this fear.

When a person falls behind on their mortgage payments, the bank will eventually send someone to the property to determine if it is still occupied. Sometimes it will be a bank employee, but in many cases it is a real estate agent or third party representative sent out to the property. If the property is deemed to be occupied, the bank will continue with the foreclosure proceeding but will not secure the house.

If the property is deemed to be vacant or abandoned, then the bank may change the locks and secure the property even though the bank does not yet own it. That may entail boarding up broken windows or winterizing the house. The mortgage lender does this to prevent further loss of value that may result from vandalism, burglary, or frozen pipes in the winter. Vacant or abandoned houses face a much higher risk of damage from theft or deferred maintenance. Mortgage lenders prefer to know that the property is occupied.

If the bank secures the property before they take it via the foreclosure process, upon request they must release the keys to the homeowner or the real estate agent for the owner. Sometimes the keys are mailed to the owner or agent. In other cases, the keys are placed in a lockbox on the premises, and the bank simply provides the code to open the lockbox. In rare circumstances, the bank may mail the wrong keys.

It is relatively common for a listing agent of a vacant house facing foreclosure to receive a call from another agent who says that the lockbox combination they were given is not working. That is a telltale sign that the lender changed the locks. The third party companies that secure properties often do not contact the owner or the listing agent.

If a homeowner facing foreclosure is going to be away from home for a time, they should inform their bank that the property is still occupied. Perhaps the owner could even post a note in the front window that would be noticeable to the bank's representative who is sent to verify occupancy.

In many cases, it is advisable for a homeowner in default to continue residing in their house for as long as possible. The homeowner will save money because they do not have to pay rent elsewhere. Also, the house maintains its value longer due to it being occupied. If the house is worth more due to it being in good condition, that means the bank will lose less money when it does sell. If the bank minimizes its losses, that makes a short sale more likely to be approved for the borrower.

CHAPTER 19. WHAT YOU NEED TO KNOW WHEN SELLING A SHORT SALE PROPERTY

If you don't like something change it; if you can't change it, change the way you think about it.

- Mary Engelbreit

Can I Sell My Short Sale Property Without a Real Estate Agent?

It is possible in some cases for someone to conduct a short sale without the involvement of real estate agents. However, it is much better for someone considering a short sale to list their property with a licensed agent.

Below are the reasons why sellers of a short sale property should work with an agent:

1. Many banks will only consider a short sale if the property is listed by a licensed agent. The banks know that an agent will be able to market the property on a wide scale. The banks also realize that agents will disclose known defects about the property. Agents will disclose to buyers that the transaction is a potential short sale. Furthermore, many agents will provide guidance to the seller on which offer to accept.

> TAI TIDBITS...
>
> If you're a short sale seller, why wouldn't you want to work with a licensed agent? Their commission is paid out of the sale proceeds, so the money is not coming out of your pocket. Besides, banks trust agents to get the best possible buyer.

2. Banks like to work with licensed agents because of the reduced potential for mortgage fraud. Licensed agents know about the basic concepts of real estate. Licensees are less likely to commit fraud, as doing so could cause them to lose their license and their livelihood. Many agents are REALTORS®, who are bound by a common Code of Ethics. All agents operate under the guidance of a broker, whose role is to ensure that transactions are conducted effectively, ethically, and legally.

3. Banks prefer to review and approve standardized real estate contracts, which agents typically use. A standardized contract is often worded with protections for buyer and seller. A standardized contract is less likely to contain hidden clauses that may create unfair advantages for the buyer or another party. Non-standard contracts created by auctioneers, attorneys, private buyers, or the sellers themselves may contain provisions (or a lack of provisions) that swing the contract totally in favor of one party.

4. Mortgage lenders may wish to talk with a listing agent about the short sale, with the expectation that the agent would be more credible than the seller. A seller might be too emotional or inexperienced to deal with the bank's negotiator.

5. Agents will qualify a buyer's ability to purchase the property. If an owner trying to sell their house themselves enters into a contract with a buyer who is not qualified, then the entire transaction is a waste of time and money.

Many owners of a short sale who have tried to sell their property themselves have found that the bank demands extensive proof that the property has been marketed effectively. Providing such proof may be difficult. Since most mortgage lenders now mandate that the property must be listed with an agent as a condition of considering a short sale, it is not worth the time and money for a seller to attempt to sell the property themselves.

In 2012, Bank of America started a program to simultaneously market selected short sale properties for sale on www.auction.com while the houses were listed with a local agent. This program allows the agent to receive their full commission as long as they hold at least two open houses in conjunction with the auction website. Nationstar Mortgage (now known as Mr. Cooper) followed suit, utilizing www.auction.com even more than Bank of America.

People who try to sell their short sale property on their own may also embroil themselves in legal liability if they fail to properly disclose the short sale nature of the transaction. A seller who unwittingly signs a contract without a short sale disclosure and/or short sale clause may be compelled to sell the house even though a short sale approval is not obtained. In other words, the seller may be contractually obligated to make up the difference themselves because they told the buyer that they would sell at a certain price by a certain date.

There are some fraudulent buyers and flippers who seek to take advantage of a naïve or unwitting short sale seller. A person trying to commit fraud may be attempting to engineer a transaction whereby the bank is deceived. Some people may attempt to lure the seller into signing over the deed or signing an option to purchase, which clouds the title and forces any end-buyer to pay the deed or option-holder money. Some people may tell the bank that their low offer is the very best price that the market will bear, only to deliberately conceal the existence of a substantially higher offer in the hopes of collecting the difference. If there were a real estate agent involved in the transaction, he or she may spot the fraudulent activity and alert the seller and perhaps others.

A short sale seller who wants to use an auctioneer may find that the highest bid price is below what a bank would accept. Furthermore, many auction companies may not want to spend advertising dollars on an auction sale that is contingent upon a short sale.

It is best for a seller of a short sale to list their property with a licensed agent.

What Asking Price Should We Choose When Listing our Short Sale Property for Sale?

A short sale listing should be listed for sale at fair market value or slightly below. The price can be lowered every three to four weeks if there is not enough interest from buyers.

It is futile to list a property too high. Some agents and sellers list the property at a ridiculously high price that would theoretically pay off the entire mortgage balance and all other closing costs. Buyers will not accidentally pay too much for a property. They typically will not even look at a property that is listed well above market value. Listing at too high a price is a waste of time.

Some agents and sellers think that the mortgage lender dictates the list price. In certain short sale programs, like the FHA Preforeclosure Sale program or Fannie Mae/Freddie Mac HAFA II program, the mortgage lender may determine

> TAI TIDBITS...
>
> Price your property to sell. An overpriced house will not attract buyers. I recommend a price reduction every three weeks. A good rule of thumb is to drop the price by five percent each time.

the list price. Some cooperative short sale programs also entail the lender choosing the list price. In traditional short sales, which comprise the majority of all short sales, the seller determines the asking price after consulting with their agent. If you're not sure, just pick the asking price. Theodore Roosevelt once said, "In any moment of decision, the best thing you can do is the right thing, the next best thing is the wrong thing, and the worst thing you can do is nothing."

Some agents list short sales well below fair market value, hoping to attract a multitude of buyers. Some agents may simply use the short sale listing to attract buyers who they will divert to other listings. The challenge with listing a property too low is that the seller's lender may be unlikely to approve a sale price substantially below fair market value. The lender will send an agent to the property to conduct a Broker's Price Opinion (BPO), or the lender might even hire an appraiser. If the lender's valuation is much higher than the sale price in the Agreement of Sale, then the sale will probably not be approved at the low price.

On a national scale, according to Zillow.com in 2012, the average short sale sells for 20 percent below fair market value. The average foreclosed home sells for 40 percent below fair market value. Nevertheless, the ultimate market value of a short sale is dependent upon local market conditions and the condition of the property. If the house is in a desirable neighborhood and it is in good shape, then the property will likely sell close to fair market value.

TAI TIDBITS...

As a short sale seller, it is better to receive 10 offers and say no versus receiving zero offers. Price your house to sell.

We Are Selling our Property Via a Short Sale and We Just Received a Low Offer. Should We Make a Counteroffer, or Will the Bank Do That?

The seller of a short sale listing has the right to make counteroffers or even reject an offer outright. If a seller receives an offer that they believe is too low for their mortgage lender to approve, then the seller may negotiate with the buyer to increase the offer price.

Some buyers will be puzzled as to why they receive a counteroffer from the seller. These buyers prefer to have the seller sign off on their low offer, take the property off the market, and submit the low offer to the bank in the hopes of a short sale approval. By accepting a low offer, the seller might be missing out on a higher, better offer from another potential buyer. Yet it is also possible that the bank might issue a short sale approval on a low offer some of the time.

If an offer price is a little low but still close to fair market value, it is advisable for the seller to accept the offer and submit it to their bank. If the bank issues a counteroffer to the buyer, the buyer will perceive that the bank is the bad guy in the negotiation process. That way the seller preserves some goodwill in the negotiation. The seller may be more likely to receive a late-stage concession from a buyer who appreciates that the seller did not make any counteroffers themselves.

If an offer price is ridiculously low, it may be best for the seller to issue a counteroffer to the buyer. If the buyer is truly interested in the property, they may come up in price.

We Received Multiple Offers for our Short Sale Listing. Should We Send All the Offers to our Bank to Decide Which One to Accept?

In a short sale, the bank is not the owner and therefore does not have the right to decide which offer to accept. The sale contract is between the seller and the buyer, not between the bank and the buyer. The seller decides which offer to accept. Once that offer is accepted, the seller and buyer are committed to each other per the terms of the agreement. The fully signed contract is then submitted to the seller's bank to see if they will be willing to accept the net proceeds of the sale. The seller is responsible for deciding which offer has the best chance of being approved for a short sale by their lender.

In some states the law requires that the lienholders be informed of all short sale offers. There have been cases where the bank's representative demands to see all the offers. In states that require that the lienholder be notified of other offers, then the lienholder does wield significant influence over which offer is acceptable for the short sale. In states like Pennsylvania that do not have such laws in place, then the lienholder only needs to see the contract that the seller signed and accepted.

If the bank has taken the property back via foreclosure, then the property is owned by the bank. The situation is no longer a short sale. The bank sells the property and therefore has the right to decide which offer to accept.

I'm Selling My House Via a Short Sale and We Are Under Contract with a Buyer. If We Receive a Higher, Better Offer, Can We Send That to the Bank?

The terms of the real estate contract must be followed. Most standard contracts commit the buyer and seller to each other, so the seller cannot arbitrarily terminate an agreement with one buyer to go with another buyer.

Generally speaking, when the parties are under contract, the seller has to sell and the buyer does not necessarily have to buy. If a buyer defaults, the remedy for the seller is that they keep the buyer's deposit. If the seller defaults, the buyer could sue for performance. In other words, the buyer could sue to compel the seller to sell the property per the terms and conditions outlined in the contract.

Typically, a seller of a short sale commits to the buyer via the signed contract. In many cases, the listing agent should mark the listing as Pending or Under Contract. The property is not actively marketed to other buyers while the buyer and seller await a short sale approval, or denial, from the seller's mortgage lender.

Think about it this way: The buyer stops searching for another property to purchase. The buyer pays for inspections and perhaps for a loan rate lock. The buyer may sell their property or terminate their lease based upon the representations of the seller. Therefore, the buyer is committed to the deal. The seller should recognize the buyer's commitment and allow the short sale approval process to play out, without planning to remove the buyer from the deal if a more enticing offer comes along.

> TAI TIDBITS...
>
> As a short sale seller, pick a committed buyer and commit to them. As a short sale buyer, pick a committed seller and commit to them. The transaction is doomed to fail if one or both parties do not show commitment in their words and actions.

Some people erroneously believe that all buyer offers, whenever they come in, should be presented to the seller's bank. The seller, as the owner of the property, chooses the one offer that they will accept. Once signed, that contract is the only one submitted to the seller's bank for a short sale approval. The bank is not the owner and does not have the authority to pick and choose among offers.

In a short sale, the buyer and seller should commit to each other. Once the seller's mortgage lender makes a decision about the short sale, then the buyer and seller can either proceed to closing or go their separate ways.

When Should Home Inspections Be Done in a Short Sale Transaction?

A matter of debate is whether a buyer should conduct their home inspection right after going under contract with a short sale seller, or if the buyer should wait until a written short sale approval is provided. In typical non-distressed sales, the buyer opts to conduct their home inspection within 10 to 15 days after all parties have signed the real estate contract. However, when a short sale is involved, there are pros and cons of conducting a home inspection right away. What is advantageous for the buyer may not be advantageous for the seller, and vice-versa.

Why a buyer should want to conduct inspections right away

- If the buyer decides from the inspection results that they do not want the property, the buyer saves valuable time by terminating the contract. They can then focus their search for a better home.

- If the buyer decides that they need a repair credit or price reduction, they have a much greater chance of having the seller's mortgage lender approve the concession. The information from the inspection report can help with convincing the seller's bank that the property needs to sell for less due to projected repairs. Once a short sale is approved, it is extremely difficult to negotiate a concession with the seller's mortgage lender.

- In many real estate contracts, the buyer may forfeit their deposit if they attempt to back out of the transaction only days before a closing is set to occur.

Why a buyer should wait until they have short sale approval before conducting inspections

- If the buyer's offer price is not approved by the seller's mortgage lender, then the buyer does not spend money on an inspection for a home they cannot buy.

- The condition of the property may deteriorate from deferred maintenance while waiting for the seller's mortgage lender to respond. The buyer's inspection report may more accurately represent the condition of the property as of the proposed settlement date.

Why a seller should want the buyer to conduct inspections right away

- If the seller takes the property off the market for months while waiting for short sale approval, the seller takes a huge risk. If the buyer terminates the contract due to inspection results, the seller will have wasted valuable marketing time. Once a short sale approval is granted and the lender expects a closing in 30 days, the likelihood of finding another buyer who can purchase the property in that time frame is slim.

- If the buyer walks away only a few days after signing the sale contract, the seller now has valuable information about the property thanks to that former buyer. That knowledge can help with the short sale negotiation with the bank. Furthermore, the listing agent may be better able to price the property in line with its condition.

Why the seller should not want the buyer to wait until they have short sale approval before conducting inspections

- If the buyer needs a mortgage loan, they may run out of time. If the seller's lender demands that the settlement occur within 30 days, and the buyer spends 15 days on inspections, it leaves only 15 days for them to obtain the mortgage loan. If there is a delay with the buyer's appraisal or their bank's underwriters, then the transaction is in jeopardy. The seller's lender may not extend the short sale approval, or if they do they'll demand extra money for every extra day. In such situations, an argument can ensue over who will pay the per diem to the seller's lender.

- The seller may have made preparations to move out, only to find that the buyer walks away just days before the projected settlement. The seller has to move out, and many people need about four weeks' notice to plan a move. If the seller's lender demands a closing in 30 days after the short sale approval is granted, and the buyer decides 15 days later to walk away, then the seller is stuck in limbo. The seller may have already begun the move-out process when they find that the buyer decides to terminate the Agreement of Sale just days before the planned closing date. Then the house will sit vacant for weeks, even months, as the listing agent works to procure a new buyer.

If either buyer or seller is not fully committed to the other party, there is a high probability that the transaction will fail. When a buyer conducts their inspections right away, it demonstrates the buyer's commitment since the buyer is willing to spend money up front. The seller in turn should feel assured that they can take the property off the market to commit to that buyer.

In my opinion, it is best for all parties to have the home inspections conducted right after signing of the contract. While the buyer has to spend several hundred dollars on inspections, that is the cost of doing business. Typically a buyer can purchase a short sale at a discount to fair market value, and that discount justifies the expenditure of money up front. In fact, the inspection results may benefit the buyer in that the report and any repair estimates can influence the seller's lender to allow the house to be sold at a discount.

When Should My Short Sale Listing Be Marked as Pending?

There are a lot of myths and resulting arguments as to when a short sale offer should be considered under contract.

The listing agent presents offers to the seller for a decision. The seller, who is the owner of record, is the one who decides which offer to accept.

In a short sale, the lender must also agree to the transaction since they are being asked to take less than what is owed. However, the bank is not the seller. The lender's acceptance or rejection of the short sale is a contingency to the contract.

When the seller signs the standard Pennsylvania Agreement of Sale, the offer is accepted, though it has the short sale contingency that must be resolved later. The real estate contract is between the buyer and the seller, not between the bank and the buyer.

Many Multiple Listing Services (MLSs) require a listing broker to change the status of a listing to pending or under contract once an offer is accepted. Even if an MLS system does not require a change in status to pending or under contract, the head broker in the listing office might have a policy requiring a status change.

Regardless of what the MLS rules are, agents are ethically required to disclose the existence of accepted offers, including those with unresolved contingencies. If another agent or buyer inquire about the property, the listing agent must inform them up front that the seller has already signed a real estate contract that is awaiting lender approval of the short sale.

Some states allow a seller to accept an offer in a backup capacity, so long as the backup buyer is fully apprised of the existence and precedence of the first accepted offer. In other words, the seller can sign another offer, but that does not override the first contract. The backup buyer can only come into the picture if the first buyer and seller terminate their contract. In Pennsylvania, it is unwise to have more than one offer signed by the seller.

Some listing brokers like to continue to show a short sale listing just in case the current buyer under contract decides to walk away. On the one hand, that is a good strategy, as many buyers may end up walking away from the deal. However, it behooves the listing broker and seller to select the right buyer in the first place, so the need for a backup buyer diminishes.

We believe that the buyer and seller should commit to the transaction. For the buyer, that means making a hefty deposit, scheduling any inspections right away, and agreeing to wait for the long term. For the seller, that includes marking the listing as being under contract.

CHAPTER 20. WHAT IF IT IS NOT MY PRINCIPAL RESIDENCE?

Thinking will not overcome fear but action will.

- W. Clement Stone

What If It Is Not My Principal Residence?

A person can still have a short sale approved even if they are not residing at the property. Some short sale programs require that the house be the borrower's primary residence, while other programs will consider a property that is vacant or occupied by someone else. Generally speaking, it is advantageous for a short sale seller in many situations to remain in the house, as many programs favor those using the property as their principal residence.

Are Short Sales Allowed on Commercial and Investment Properties?

A short sale can be conducted on any type of property. If the seller owes more than the property is worth, and the mortgage lender is willing to take less than what is owed, then a short sale can occur. Short sales can occur with one's primary residence, a vacation home, a commercial property, a multi-unit property, or vacant land.

In any short sale, if the mortgage lender forgives the remaining debt, the former borrower can expect to receive a 1099-C Cancellation of Debt form the following January. The forgiven debt will be reported to the Internal Revenue Service. If the property was an investment property, second home, vacant land, or a commercial property, then the former borrower will likely have to pay some tax on the forgiven debt. The IRS has historically treated forgiven debt as ordinary income.

If a person sells their primary residence via a short sale, they may not have to pay any income tax. The Mortgage Forgiveness Debt Relief Act of 2007 applied to debt forgiven in calendar years 2007 through 2017. Up to $2 million of forgiven debt is eligible for this exclusion ($1 million if married filing separately). Debt reduced through mortgage restructuring, as well as mortgage debt forgiven in connection with a foreclosure, may qualify for this relief. In most cases, eligible homeowners only need to fill out a few lines on IRS Form 982. Congressman Ron Kind of

Wisconsin introduced a bill in March 2019 to extend the debt relief through the end of 2019.

The debt must have been used to buy, build, or substantially improve the taxpayer's principal residence and must have been secured by that residence. Debt used to refinance qualifying debt is also eligible for the exclusion, but only up to the amount of the old mortgage principal, just before the refinancing.

Will the Bank Forgive My Debt on a Commercial Property or Vacation Home?

Everything in real estate is negotiable, although some things are far more negotiable than others. Many lenders are willing to forgive the remaining debt on short sales involving commercial properties, vacation homes, and multi-unit buildings. The decision whether to forgive the debt or pursue the seller for a deficiency judgment is up to the lender. If the bank believes that the seller is destitute, then it does not make good business sense for them to spend thousands of dollars trying to collect money from someone who does not have it.

The bigger issue for a short sale seller of a commercial property, second home, or investment building may be the tax consequence of the forgiven debt.

If a business owner has $200,000 of debt forgiven on a commercial building, then that owner will probably be liable for paying income tax on that $200,000. If the phantom income, as it is called, is not offset by losses or expenses, then there will be a hefty tax due. $200,000 of added income in a 25 percent tax bracket means that the person could owe $50,000 to the IRS. Anyone considering a short sale should consult with their advisors about the potential tax consequences.

CHAPTER 21: WHAT IS A BPO AND WHY IS IT SO CRITICAL TO MY SHORT SALE?

There is a tendency at every important but difficult crossroad to pretend that it's not really there.

- Bill McKibben

My Bank Is Sending Someone Over for a BPO. What Should I Do?

The Broker's Price Opinion (BPO) is perhaps the most critical step in the short sale approval process. A BPO is the bank's field review of the property to determine the basis for its value.

A lender will typically approve a mortgage payoff that is a predetermined percentage of the BPO value. For example, a lender might only allow a payoff of no less than 84 percent of the value established in the BPO report. In other words, if the BPO states that the property is worth $100,000, then the lender might expect to receive no less than $84,000. That does not mean the lender would approve a sale price of $84,000. Adding realty commission, closing costs, and property taxes on top of that, it is feasible the lender would accept a sale price of $92,000 or higher.

So, if the Agreement of Sale price is $105,000 and the BPO values the property at $100,000, the bank will be eager to approve a short sale at $105,000. If the BPO values the property at $100,000 but the price in the Agreement of Sale is $60,000, the bank will likely reject that sale price. Therefore, it is important that the BPO valuation be reasonably close to the sale price.

The lender often hires a real estate agent from the area to perform the valuation. In some cases, the agent may not be from the area. Furthermore, the agent may not be aware that the property is a short sale. In some situations, the bank will pay for an appraiser to conduct an appraisal, but the lender may still refer to the report as a BPO.

A short sale seller does not need to tidy up the house for the BPO agent. The seller does not need to leave the house, as this is not a normal showing with a buyer. The BPO agent will take exterior photos and in most cases, interior photos. The seller, or the listing agent, should point out the defects and necessary repairs for inclusion in the report that goes to the bank. The BPO agent should be informed that this is a short sale situation. The cause of the hardship should be conveyed.

It is okay for the listing agent to give a few comparable sales to the BPO agent, and many will appreciate that gesture as it can save them time in preparing the report. The listing agent should tell the BPO agent the sale price.

The objective is to inform the BPO agent of the circumstances of the sale, with the hope that their valuation will be in line with the sale price. If the BPO valuation is close to the sale price, then the bank is far more likely to approve the short sale.

If you are the listing agent, you should be involved in every aspect regarding the BPO. You should be the point of contact that the BPO agent calls to gain entry to the property.

What a Listing Agent Should Bring to the BPO Appointment:

1. The comparable sales that you believe indicate the current value of the property.

2. The listing detail report from the Multiple List Service (MLS).

3. A list of needed repairs, supported by estimate(s).

4. Copies of code violations or other notices.

5. Copy of the seller's hardship letter.

6. The listing history, to show price reductions over time. If possible, also include a list of prior showings and negative feedback from those who viewed the property.

7. A description of the neighborhood and its demographics. Include a printout of a map showing the area.

8. Anything else that justifies the offer price that was submitted to the lender.

Explain to the BPO agent why the offer for the property is the best possible offer. The BPO agent is typically paid $30.00 to $95.00 to conduct the report.

Bring a cold bottle of water or soda for the BPO agent. Strike up a good rapport and help make their job easier. If you're convincing enough, the BPO might come in at the number that you need to make the short sale work.

Some banks are hiring appraisers but still referring to the report as a BPO. In Pennsylvania, agents are technically not permitted to conduct a "BPO" unless they meet specific educational requirements, but they are allowed to generate a Comparable Market Analysis (CMA) for a client or prospective client. Nevertheless, the bank will probably refer to the valuation report as a "BPO," regardless of whether it is a CMA, BPO, or appraisal.

Most of the time, the mortgage lender will not reveal the exact valuation from the BPO or appraisal. They do not have to tell you the amount. If the loan negotiator refuses to tell you what the valuation was, you may be able to figure it out. Ask a question like, "How close is the BPO amount to the offer price?" or "How reasonable is the offer price compared to the BPO amount?" or "What price range did the BPO amount come in at?"

Wait a Minute, are BPOs Allowed in Pennsylvania?

The Pennsylvania Real Estate Commission states that a real estate licensee may conduct a BPO for a lender if the licensee meets certain educational requirements and has their Broker of Record sign off on the report. Other states have differing definitions and/or restrictions regarding BPOs, what they are, and who may create them.

The phrase "BPO" has become commonplace in the banking industry. Every bank we have worked with utilizes that term. Sometimes the BPO they speak of is an appraisal, sometimes it is a BPO (via the Pennsylvania Real Estate Commission definition), and sometimes it is a CMA. The bank representatives simply say, "We ordered a BPO" or "We're waiting for the BPO to come back."

By my observation, I have observed more and more banks paying for bona fide appraisals (while still calling them a "BPO").

Nevertheless, there are numerous licensees out there who prepare BPOs. Some Pennsylvania licensees call them a CMA but the bank that hired them calls it a BPO. We know because we've seen situations where a bank told agents to send them a BPO and they told the bank that in Pennsylvania, we only do CMAs. The lender representative didn't care what the agents called it; he simply wanted a report with sold comparables and active listings.

In our opinion, it would exhaust one's time and resources to insist that all BPOs be conducted by a broker, appraiser, or licensee who has met the state educational requirements. It would also be too much to try to convince banks to refer to those reports as CMAs.

We believe the focus should be on communicating to the agent/broker/appraiser that this is a short sale, that there is a hardship, and that this is a distressed sale in which other distressed comparables should be considered for the report.

CHAPTER 22. ASSET PROTECTION: WHAT THE BANK CAN AND CANNOT TAKE FROM YOU

Sleep, riches, and health to be truly enjoyed must be interrupted.

- Johann Paul Friedrich Richter

Can the Bank Sue Me After a Sheriff's Sale?

Yes, but they are unlikely to actually do so. Technically a mortgage lender can pursue the former homeowner for the remainder of the debt even though the house was taken back by the bank at the Sheriff's Sale. The lender could also sue the former borrower after a deed-in-lieu of foreclosure if there was no settlement reached regarding the remaining debt. The lawsuit has to be initiated within six months. Once started, the lender can pursue the borrower for up to 20 years.

I Need a Short Sale on One Property of Mine. Can the Bank Go After My Other House?

The mortgage given by the owner to the bank gives the bank the right to take ownership of the house via the foreclosure process if the owner does not pay. The mortgage lender's remedy is to take ownership of the house so it can be sold to recoup some or all of the defaulted loan.

The bank cannot seize other real estate owned by the borrower unless the borrower has some type of blanket mortgage loan that applies to more than one property. Most mortgage loans are not blanket loans but simply a loan secured by one property.

In some cases and in some states, the mortgage lender can foreclose on the borrower and may sue the borrower after the sale if the lender did not recoup the balance of the loan. In other words, if the bank foreclosed and found that the value of the property is far below what they are owed, they can pursue the former owner for some or all of the remaining balance. If the bank sues and is granted a deficiency judgment, then the former owner has to pay off that judgment somehow. The payment of that judgment may come when the person sells another one of their properties.

Although some states restrict the collection of deficiency balances, most states including Pennsylvania have laws that permit deficiencies to be treated like other unsecured debts. In states that allow deficiency judgments, the lender may be able to garnish the borrower's wages, levy their bank accounts, and/or place a lien on other real estate they own.

In some short sales, the bank desires to retain the right to pursue a deficiency judgment after the sale of the property. The mortgage lender should declare that intention on their short sale approval letter. The borrower has the right to reject that condition of the short sale, and the parties may re-negotiate. The borrower may propose that the bank forgive the remaining debt instead of pursuing the deficiency judgment.

States with anti-deficiency laws are Alaska, Arizona, California, Iowa, Minnesota, Montana, North Carolina, North Dakota, Oregon, and Washington. It should be noted that some of these states allow deficiency lawsuits in certain situations. These anti-deficiency laws are rarely straightforward.

In rare cases, the bank may be willing to release its lien on one property to allow a short sale to occur, but the bank will add a lien to another property as long as the owner consents. This tactic is more prevalent with local banks instead of national banks. The parties negotiate a deal whereby the seller allows the bank to place a mortgage against another property for the amount of the loan that remains unpaid by the short sale. This may be a wise tactic for the seller if they have equity in one property but no equity in another.

In a Short Sale, Can My Mortgage Lender Go After My Retirement Account?

Typically, no, the mortgage lender cannot lay claim to the assets in one's retirement account. I have been involved in hundreds of short sales, and I have never seen a mortgage lender claim any funds out of a seller's retirement account.

There are ways that the retirement account can affect whether one is approved for a short sale. In making their decision on whether to approve a short sale, a lender may note how much money is in the retirement account and then ask the seller to sign a promissory note to repay some of the debt. Even though the lender does not ask for a monetary contribution from the seller at settlement, and even though the lender agrees to forgive most of the remaining debt, they may expect the seller to repay some debt in the future. The promissory notes we have seen typically do not involve any interest, and they have ranged from as little as $1,000 to as high as

$40,000. In other words, the lender knows that the borrower does not have funds now but could have access to retirement funds in the future.

A person's retirement funds could be indirectly affected by the filing of a judgment. For example, if a lender obtains a deficiency judgment against a former borrower, that judgment sits on the public record for a time, and it can be renewed by the lender. Eventually, if the person wants to borrow money or sell a house in the county where the judgment is filed, they probably will have to pay off the judgment or reach a settlement agreement to remove the judgment. The person could potentially use money disbursed from their retirement account to pay off the judgment. A factor to consider is how many years away from retirement the person is, as someone closer to retirement has to deal with the possibility of having a judgment that they may wish to pay off.

In theory, a lender could issue a short sale approval and ask the borrower to contribute some money at closing. The lender may be aware that the person has no liquid funds but has some funds in their retirement account. Some accounts allow a person to remove some money, but it comes with a penalty. Therefore, it is possible that a borrower may choose to have their retirement fund release some money early just so the person can cover a contribution at closing and perhaps their moving costs.

It is important to understand that the mortgage lender's remedy for a defaulted mortgage loan is to foreclose on the property. The lender's claim is against the property, not against the person's retirement account. If the person needs money and chooses to take some funds from the retirement account to cover immediate expenses, then that is their choice and not the lender's decision.

State laws can vary regarding a creditor's claim to personal assets. Consult with your attorney and/or tax advisor.

CHAPTER 23. LANDLORD-TENANT ISSUES WITH SHORT SALES

Life is difficult for everyone; everyone has bad days. Everyone has trouble in their life, because it doesn't matter how rich you are: Sickness and trouble and worry and love, these things will mess with you at every level of life.

- Domhnail Gleeson

If a Tenant Resides in a Property That Is Foreclosed, Does the Lease Survive the Foreclosure Action?

Each state has its own laws to govern the rights of tenants if a house is foreclosed. In Pennsylvania, tenants in a foreclosed house may stay at least 30 days after the Sheriff's Sale. The law allows the tenants to stay 30 days. The law also states that the new owner must obtain an ejectment action against the occupants through the courts before the occupants can be removed.

Some lenders are offering tenants the opportunity to continue living in a foreclosed house as long as they pay rent under a new lease agreement with the lender. However, in the majority of cases, the lender seeks to eject the occupant because their goal is to sell the house.

Can a Landlord Facing Foreclosure Still Collect Rent from the Tenant?

Yes, a landlord who has not paid the mortgage may continue to collect rent from the tenant. Many mortgage lenders have an Assignment of Rents clause in the note, whereby the mortgage company has the right to receive the rent when the loan is in default. In actual practice, I have not seen the Assignment of Rents clause exercised on residential properties.

The lease will lay out the duties and expectations of the landlord and the tenant. If the landlord fulfills their duties, such as keeping the property maintained, the tenant has to pay rent. If the landlord breaches the lease, the tenant can take the landlord to court to resolve the problem or obtain some relief for the breach.

I've seen several cases where the tenant stopped paying the rent when they realized the landlord was not paying the mortgage. The landlord took the tenant to court for non-payment of rent. I've seen the judge rule that the tenant must be evicted since they failed to pay the rent. However, the judge also ruled that the landlord would not receive a judgment against the tenant for the unpaid rent.

What Rights Do Tenants Have in a Foreclosed Home?

The federal Protecting Tenants at Foreclosure Act (PTFA) of 2009 provided additional protections for certain tenants in a foreclosed residential property. The PTFA was effective from May 20, 2009 until December 31, 2014.

Under the now-expired PTFA, tenants with a bona fide lease that was signed before a notice of foreclosure could reside in a foreclosed home under the terms of their lease for at least 90 days. The new owner had to give a notice to vacate to the tenant at least 90 days in advance of the termination date. The tenant had to pay rent under the terms of their lease, although the rent will be paid to the new owner after the date of the foreclosure sale. Some states provide additional protections to tenants in foreclosed homes.

A bona fide lease was defined in the PTFA as one in which:

- The tenant is not the borrower or the child, spouse, or parent of the borrower.

- The lease or tenancy was the result of an arms-length transaction in which neither landlord nor tenant has a familial or prior business relationship.

- The rent is an amount considered to be fair market rent or close to it, or the unit's rent is subsidized by local, state, or federal funds.

With the expiration of the PTFA at the end of 2014, consumer advocates expected an increase in evictions. The country's largest mortgage servicer, Wells Fargo, announced it is no longer following the guidelines from the Act. J.P. Morgan Chase, CitiGroup, and Nationstar continue to adhere to the guidelines. (Berry, 2015)

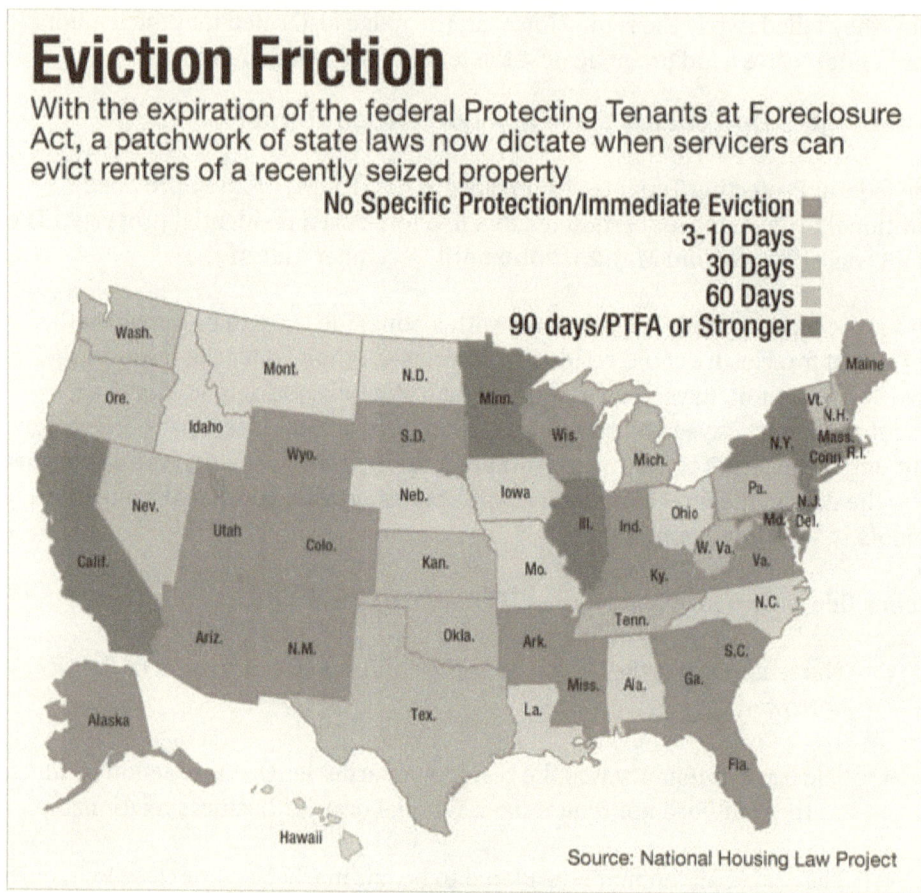

Eviction Friction

With the expiration of the federal Protecting Tenants at Foreclosure Act, a patchwork of state laws now dictate when servicers can evict renters of a recently seized property

No Specific Protection/Immediate Eviction
3-10 Days
30 Days
60 Days
90 days/PTFA or Stronger

Source: National Housing Law Project

Per the National Low Income Housing Coalition, only nine states and the District of Columbia have laws that match or exceed the provisions of the PTFA. Eight states allow for the immediate eviction of tenants. Nineteen states have no specific protections for tenants in a home that is facing foreclosure. Three states calls for 60 days' notice, and eight states require notice in the range of 3 to 30 days before eviction can occur. (National Low Income Housing Coalition, 2015)

CHAPTER 24. I'M ON THE DEED BUT NOT ON THE MORTGAGE. WILL THE MORTGAGE COMPANY COME AFTER ME?

There are uses to adversity, and they don't reveal themselves until tested. Whether it's serious illness, financial hardship, or the simple constraint of parents who speak limited English, difficulty can tap unexpected strengths.

- Sonia Sotomayor

There are situations where not all of the people on the deed are on the mortgage too. The lender can pursue the people who signed the mortgage and note. All of the owners of record will be notified about the foreclosure sale.

Below are examples of actual situations I have seen. The names have been changed to protect the parties.

Wife later added to deed but not the mortgage

John Doe borrowed money from a mortgage lender to purchase his home. A couple of years later, John married Jane. John decided to add Jane's name to the deed, so they could both be official owners of the property. John and Jane then fell upon hard times, and they defaulted on John's mortgage loan. John received numerous collection calls at the phone numbers he had registered with his lender. John's credit score was severely damaged by the mortgage default, but Jane's credit score was unaffected.

The lender entered a Default Judgment against John in the county court. John and Jane both received notices of the foreclosure sale. When the house was foreclosed, John and Jane had to move out. John permanently has a foreclosure against his record, and on future loan applications John has to disclose the foreclosure. Jane has no foreclosure against her record, and on future loan applications Jane can report that she was never foreclosed upon.

Divorce

Joe and Sue Smith borrowed money from a mortgage lender to purchase their home, and both of their names went on the deed. A few years later, Joe and Sue decided to divorce each other. As part of the divorce agreement, Sue was allowed to

111

continue residing in the house and Joe removed his name from the deed. The divorce agreement also called for Sue to remove Joe's name from the mortgage and note. However, the mortgage lender would not simply remove Joe's name. The lender told Sue that she had to pay off the loan in full or refinance to a new loan in her own name that would pay off the old loan. Unfortunately, property values dropped and Sue's income was not sufficient to qualify for a loan.

For the time being, Sue decided to continue paying on the existing loan. Unfortunately, Sue could not maintain the payments, and the loan went into default. Both Joe and Sue received collection calls from the lender. Both Joe and Sue had default judgments entered against them.

Joe tried to explain to the lender that he had no more ownership or interest in the house, but the lender replied that he was still a guarantor. The credit scores for Joe and Sue went down. Eventually, the lender foreclosed, and both Joe and Sue had a foreclosure against their record.

Straw party

Francis had a low credit score, so he convinced his friend James to sign for a mortgage loan. James purchased the house in his name, and Francis moved in. Francis made a payment every month to James, who then paid the mortgage company. Since they were friends, they had no written agreement between them.

One day, Francis was stunned to be served with a foreclosure notice. Francis learned that for the past year, James had not paid the mortgage even though Francis had been making payments to him. James had been ignoring the collection calls from the lender all that time.

Francis tried to call the lender to ask them to transfer the loan into his name, but the lender would not even talk to Francis. Francis asked James to try for a loan modification, but the lender stated that they were too far along in the foreclosure process. The lender foreclosed on the house, and Francis was evicted. Francis and James did not talk to each other after that.

Improvements to house

Sally obtained a mortgage loan and purchased a fixer-upper. She did some of the work herself over time as she lived at the house. Unfortunately, the work she did was not up to code, and she had a lot of unfinished projects. Sally ran out of money and could no longer pay for repairs. She fell behind on her mortgage payments.

Sally approached her friend Fred, who was a handyman. Sally told Fred that if he paid for materials and finished the renovation, then Sally would sell her house and give him half the profit. Fred began work, repairing the shoddy improvements that Sally had already made in addition to handling some of the other projects.

One day while working at the house, a Sheriff's deputy handed Fred a notice of a foreclosure sale. The notice stated that the sale date was the following month. Fred was stunned and approached Sally. Sally said she would call a real estate agent to quickly sell the house.

The agent told Sally that property values had dropped in the area, and that the fair market value was below the amount that Sally owed to her mortgage lender. The agent added that it was unrealistic to sell the house in a month. Sally listed the house with the agent as a short sale, but no offers came in that month.

Fred realized that all the materials he had installed at the house, and all his labor, were essentially lost. The buyer of the house at the foreclosure auction received the benefit of all the improvements. Fred and Sally never talked again.

CHAPTER 25. HOW TO INTERPRET A SHORT SALE APPROVAL LETTER

Our very survival depends on our ability to stay awake, to adjust to new ideas, to remain vigilant and to face the challenge of change.

- Martin Luther King, Jr.

My Lender Approved the Short Sale but They Want Me to Sign a Promissory Note to Pay Some of the Remaining Debt. What Are My Options?

This happens in some short sales. Either the lender or the mortgage insurance company will grant approval of the short sale and they'll forgive most of the debt, but they'll want the seller to sign a promissory note to repay some of the remaining balance. I have seen promissory notes range from $1,000 to $40,000. Many of the promissory notes charge no interest at all. The entire payment goes toward principal.

There are several options for a seller who receives a short sale approval where they are asked to sign a promissory note as part of the deal. Below are the options:

1. **Refuse to sign the promissory note and allow the property to be foreclosed.** In many states including Pennsylvania, the lender could foreclose and pursue the borrower after the sale for some or all off the remaining balance. Some owners take a chance when they allow the lender to foreclose, and those owners hope the lender will not come after them for the balance. Foreclosure is more damaging than a short sale with regarding to one's credit and ability to obtain future loans.

2. **Refuse to sign the promissory note and renegotiate.** There are instances where a lender or mortgage insurer might consider removing the stipulation for the promissory note. Sometimes raising the sale price might work. Sometimes offering a lump sum paid at closing instead of a promissory note for a larger amount might do the trick. For example, instead of signing a $10,000 promissory note, perhaps the seller might offer to pay $2,500 at closing. Sometimes the lender or mortgage insurer might be willing to take less money now than hope to be paid more in the future.

114

3. **Sign the promissory note and make the payments.** Some people agree to make the payments since they are having most of the debt forgiven while achieving their goal of selling the house. The monthly payments on promissory notes are typically affordable.

4. **Sign the promissory note and not make the payments.** Some people choose to sign the promissory note to move forward with the short sale, and later on they do not pay the promissory note. It may be advantageous to avoid the foreclosure and agree to the promissory note, as the owner will no longer be liable for the house or a much larger debt obligation. Furthermore, avoiding foreclosure is much better for the seller if they have plans to borrow money in the future. The promissory note is an unsecured debt, so defaulting on it does not constitute a foreclosure. It will be harder for the note holder to collect on the note since it is unsecured. Some sellers plan to declare bankruptcy after the short sale, so the bankruptcy may wipe out the unsecured debt of the promissory note. It is possible for the note holder to file a judgment against the borrower. It may also be possible for the borrower to negotiate a settlement payment on the promissory note for less than the full balance.

5. **Consider a deed-in-lieu of foreclosure.** Also known as a friendly foreclosure, a deed-in-lieu of foreclosure involves the lender taking back the property prior to a foreclosure auction. However, a deed-in-lieu of foreclosure must be carefully negotiated, as some lenders will reserve their right to pursue the seller for the entire remaining balance of the mortgage. Some lenders may not be willing to take the property back via a deed-in-lieu of foreclosure. In some cases, a promissory note will still be expected from the borrower.

How Do I Know If the Lender is Forgiving the Remaining Debt?

Each lender has a different type of short sale approval letter. Some are one page long, and others may be 10 pages long.

Below are phrases that indicate the remaining debt is being forgiven:

- "Under this Bank of America Cooperative Short Sale Agreement, Bank of America and/or its investors and/or insurers will accept less than the payoff balance on the above referenced property and release you from any further financial responsibility for the outstanding first lien mortgage."

- "JPMorgan Chase Bank, N.A. agrees to release its security interests to the above collateral AND forgive any deficiency balances upon receipt of $112,168.12 in certified U.S. funds."

- "The owner of your mortgage note, the mortgage insurer (if your loan is covered by mortgage insurance), waive their right to pursue collection of any deficiency following the completion of your short sale and your debt is considered valid."

- "PNC Bank, N.A. will not pursue collection of the remaining deficiency balance ('Debt Forgiveness') after the closing, which after receipt of the Proceeds of Sale will be approximately $8,931.29."

- "Upon receipt of certified funds, the debt will be considered to be fully satisfied for less than the amount due and no remaining deficiency balance will be owed."

Below are phrases that indicate the remaining debt is not being forgiven:

- "Upon receipt of the funds, we also agree to release our interest in the subject property by satisfaction of the lien of record. Acceptance of this offer does not relieve the borrowers of their financial obligations of the loan deficiency and any derogatory credit reporting that may arise from it."

- "We agree to release the lien but not the underlying note."

- "The Bank is willing to accommodate the Borrower in releasing the Mortgage, provided that the Borrower affirms its obligation to pay the outstanding balance due, including principal, interest and any other charges, under the Note, after applying the 'Required Proceeds', as defined herein, to the obligations under the Note, and further provided that the Borrower otherwise fully abides by all of the terms and conditions of this Agreement. The Borrower acknowledges and affirms that following application of the Required Proceeds, the Borrower shall remain fully obligated to pay the Deficiency that shall remain due and owing under the Note, and that the Note and the Borrower's obligations thereunder shall remain in full force and effect notwithstanding the release of the Mortgage by the Bank."

CHAPTER 26. HOW DOES THE SHERIFF'S SALE WORK?

Fear stifles our thinking and actions. It creates indecisiveness that results in stagnation. I have known talented people who procrastinate indefinitely rather than risk failure. Lost opportunities cause erosion of confidence, and the downward spiral begins.

- Charles Stanley

How Long Does It Take for a Bank to Foreclose once I Stop Making Payments?

The average time to foreclose on a property has increased across the country. Banks, courts, foreclosure attorneys, and Sheriff's Departments have become inundated. Borrowers are attempting loan modifications, short sales, and other programs which typically delay the foreclosure process. Banks have sometimes delayed sales to maintain good public relations. For example, many banks choose to suspend foreclosure sales around Christmas. Other banks have placed a temporary moratorium on foreclosures due to complaints by borrowers, state governments, or others. In addition, an increasing number of borrowers choose to contest the foreclosure action against them, which delays the foreclosure sale.

How Will I Know If a Pennsylvania Sheriff's Sale or Tax Sale of My House Has Been Scheduled?

According to Rule 2958.2 of the Pennsylvania Code, written notice of a Sheriff's Sale or Tax Sale must be served upon the defendant (the borrower) at least 30 days prior to the sale date. In almost all cases, an owner will know about a sale at least 30 days in advance. The Sheriff's Department in many Pennsylvania counties will provide more than 30 days' notice.

There are numerous requirements for notifying the owner and the general public about a Sheriff's Sale or Tax Sale. Below is the complete list of notices that must be made:

- The Sheriff's office must post a notice of the sale in their office at least 30 days before the sale.

118

- The Sheriff's office must post a notice of the sale upon the property at least 30 days before the sale.

- The sale date must be published for three consecutive weeks in one newspaper of general circulation in the county. The first publication must be at least 21 days before the sale date.

- The sale date must be published in the county legal publication, if there is one. The first publication must be made at least 21 days before the sale date.

- Notice must be delivered to the borrower(s) and the owner(s) of the property. The notice can be served upon a competent adult at the residence(s) of the borrower(s) and owner(s). Alternately, the notice can be sent by certified mail to the borrower(s) and owner(s).

In some cases, not all of the owners signed a mortgage and note with the lender. Even though some owners may not owe money to the lender, the house can still be foreclosed.

The foreclosure sale or tax sale will not come as a surprise, as the owner will have at least 30 days' notice. In most cases, they will be given even more than 30 days' notice.

If I Avoid the Sheriff's Deputies, Will That Delay the Foreclosure Sale?

Yes, avoiding the Sheriff's deputies when they are delivering notice of the foreclosure sale can delay the sale for a month or more. If the Sheriff's deputies cannot locate the foreclosure defendant in person or by mail, then per Rule 430 of the Pennsylvania Code they must conduct a good faith effort to find the defendant. That includes making inquiries with the postal service, friends, relatives, and co-workers along with examining the local telephone directories, motor vehicle bureau, voter registration records, and property tax records. If the Sheriff's department made such a good faith effort and still cannot find the defendant to serve notice, then they may appeal to the court for a Special Order. The court can then authorize the Sheriff's Sale.

Can the Bank Foreclose in the Middle of Winter?

A mortgage lender can foreclose at any time of year if they have properly followed the state's foreclosure procedure. A borrower in default receives notice of the foreclosure sale well in advance. Furthermore, even after the house has been foreclosed, the occupants have some time to move out.

In recent years, major banks have elected not to foreclose on people in December since it is close to the holidays. It can create bad press for a lender to foreclose on a family right around the holidays. Some lenders will delay December foreclosures until January.

Some states have laws about eviction of families with young children in the midst of winter. Some state laws extend the time period for a family to move out during the winter months.

CHAPTER 27. CAN A PENNSYLVANIA SHERIFF'S SALE BE DELAYED?

I'm interested in that thing that happens where there's a breaking point for some people and not for others. You go through such hardship, things that are almost impossibly difficult, and there's no sign that it's going to get any better, and that's the point when people quit. But some don't.

- Robert Redford

Yes, a Pennsylvania Sheriff's Sale can be delayed either at the request of the lender or upon a stay granted by a judge. The Sheriff's Sale can be delayed up to one hour before the bidding at a foreclosure sale.

The common technique to delay a Sheriff's Sale is to convince the foreclosing mortgage lender to request it. In many cases, though not all, a lender will delay a Sheriff's Sale to allow a short sale to reach settlement.

Sometimes a lender will only initiate their request to stay the Sheriff's Sale a mere two to three days before the sale date. The bank does this just in case the short sale transaction is not working out to their satisfaction, so they can quickly go ahead with the foreclosure sale if necessary. The risk to sellers and agents is that if the left hand does not know what the right hand is doing, the bank's attorney or the Sheriff's auctioneer might not receive the message to delay the sale. Unfortunately, we have seen this happen on numerous occasions.

Once the Sheriff's Sale occurs, it is final. There is no right of redemption in Pennsylvania like there is in some other states.

Another method of delaying a Sheriff's Sale is for the borrower to declare bankruptcy. A bankruptcy will postpone the foreclosure sale until the trustee or presiding judge releases the real estate from the bankruptcy proceeding. We have seen borrowers declare bankruptcy a mere hour before a Sheriff's Sale. In those cases, they have been able to delay the foreclosure action for months while the bankruptcy runs its course.

One other technique to delay a Sheriff's Sale is for the borrower or their representative to convince a judge to grant a stay or continuance. Sometimes a judge will delay a Sheriff's Sale to allow for a possible conciliation. We have seen

121

various judges grant continuances from 30 days to six months. The borrower may file a petition seeking relief from the judgment or a delay of the Sheriff's Sale. Rule 2965 of the Pennsylvania Code states that the petition must be filed within 30 days after the date the Default Judgment is served to the borrower or they may lose their rights to file. We have seen some cases where a petition filed more than 30 days later was considered valid enough to convince a judge to postpone the Sheriff's Sale.

In rare cases, the Sheriff's department will postpone a foreclosure sale due to a high volume of cases.

What is the Difference Between a Sheriff's Sale Being Stayed Versus Continued?

In each Pennsylvania county, a monthly Sheriff's Sale is held to auction off properties facing foreclosure. A property scheduled for a Sheriff's Sale could potentially be "stayed" or "continued." If a property is stayed, it means that the court order requiring the property to be sold at auction has been cancelled. This can happen for a variety of reasons, such as the owner paying off the entire balance, a loan modification being reached, or a short sale agreement being negotiated. If the owner's objective is to avoid the foreclosure auction, then they would prefer to hear that their Sheriff's Sale has been stayed versus continued.

If a property is "postponed" or "continued," it means that the sale of the property has been rescheduled to a future date. The Sheriff's Department and/or auctioneer must declare what date the property will again be placed up for auction, which in many cases is the following month's Sheriff's Sale.

CHAPTER 28. WHAT HAPPENS AFTER THE SHERIFF'S SALE?

The real measure of your wealth is how much you'd be worth if you lost all your money.

- Bernard Meltzer

What Is Cash for Keys?

Cash for keys is a situation where the new owner, typically the bank that foreclosed, pays the occupant a few hundred to a few thousand dollars to move out so the bank can take possession of the property. Cash for keys may save a bank the time, money, and hassle of going through the courts to evict the occupant. In some situations, the only reason the occupant continues to reside in the house is because they do not have enough money to move. Some lenders realize that the occupant needs enough money for a moving truck, a security deposit, and one to two months' rent at an apartment.

The lender may send their real estate agent or maintenance person to the house to negotiate with the occupant. The lender may also hire an attorney to communicate with the resident. Typically, the bank will mail a letter to the house or have someone post a notice.

Some lenders are willing to negotiate the amount of the cash for keys settlement. For instance, a lender may offer $2,000 to the person in the house, but they might be willing to go up to $4,000 if the person negotiates further. If you are in the tough position of living in a recently foreclosed home, it may be worthwhile to negotiate a little. Just be careful not to play hardball with the lender, because they could simply file for eviction and potentially even obtain a judgment of some sort. And remember that the person the lender sends to the house may be a real estate agent or maintenance person who does not work directly for the bank. Be cordial with them because they may be your biggest advocate in the cash for keys negotiation.

My House in Pennsylvania Was Foreclosed. How Many Days Can I Stay in the House Until I'm Kicked Out?

If a property in Pennsylvania is sold at the Sheriff's Sale to the highest bidder or taken back by the mortgage lender, then the new owner cannot simply change the locks or throw the occupants out on the street. The new owner must go to court and file an Action in Ejectment. It is often referred to as an eviction. The Action in Ejectment is a separate legal proceeding from the foreclosure process.

A notice of the Action in Ejectment, known as a complaint, will be delivered to the occupants. The former borrower has 20 days to respond to the notice. If they do not contest the ejectment action, then the new owner will be granted possession. They must then contact the Sheriff's department to schedule the date of ejectment, which should occur within 90 days but typically 30 days.

If the former borrower or the occupant of the property (sometimes a tenant) disputes the Action in Ejectment, then a hearing will be scheduled. We have seen one case where the former owner lived in the house for 13 months after the Sheriff's Sale, while they contested the new owner's right to own the property.

Typically, the new owner must file the deed prior to being awarded the ejectment against the occupant. Some Sheriff's departments are so backed up that it may take months for the filing of the Sheriff's Deed.

On the date of the ejectment, the new owner must provide a locksmith to change the locks. The new owner will be expected to remove the personal property left on the premises, but the items must be temporarily stored with reasonable care. The new owner will have to provide notice to the occupant that their personal property is held in storage so they have the opportunity to retrieve their belongings. If the notice is provided but the items are not retrieved, the new owner could discard or sell the personal property after at least 30 days.

CHAPTER 29. I'M BUYING A SHORT SALE. WHAT SHOULD I KNOW?

One of the greatest discoveries a man makes, one of his great surprises, is to find he can do what he was afraid he couldn't do.

- Henry Ford

What Are the Risks in Buying a Short Sale?

Many short sales involve sellers who are financially struggling. That typically means the seller cut back on maintenance in recent months or years, so the property likely requires some work. For example, the seller may not have serviced the furnace, cleaned the gutters, or fixed broken items.

In a short sale transaction, a seller typically will not or cannot pay for repairs that may be customarily expected of non-distressed sellers. The property in most short sales is conveyed As-Is. A seller may even have difficulty paying for a use and occupancy certificate inspection with the municipality or a resale certificate from a Homeowners Association (HOA).

The buyer of a short sale may end up being expected to pay for municipal inspections, HOA resale fees, repairs, and other costs. In some cases, neither buyer nor seller will pay for something like a municipal inspection, with the expectation that the buyer will handle the municipal inspection later. However, if the municipal inspection discovers violations of existing code, then the buyer takes on the cost and responsibility of correcting the violations.

In some short sales, the seller may not have the utilities turned on for the buyer's home inspection. The buyer may be expected to incur the cost and time of activating the utilities or de-winterizing the property. If the buyer does not turn on the utilities, their property inspection will be limited in scope.

In the midst of winter, buyers have to be careful about damage from frozen pipes. If the seller stops paying for heat and does not winterize the house, the pipes could freeze. The damage could occur after the buyer's home inspection but before the settlement. If the utilities are off at the time of the closing, it may be worthwhile for the buyer to turn on the utilities and heat prior to the purchase.

Some short sales may involve trash or junk left behind. The seller may not have the money or the motivation to clean out the property.

Short sales do involve the conveyance of the property with clear and marketable title. A buyer of a short sale is strongly encouraged to pay for title insurance. Title agencies offer enhanced title insurance, which costs only 10 percent more than standard title insurance. We recommend that buyers of distressed property pay for enhanced title insurance.

Many short sales involve increased risk for the buyer. Many short sales are sold below fair market value. Therefore, buyers often pay less for a short sale in exchange for the risk they incur.

Five Things Buyers Need to Know When Purchasing a Short Sale.

1. **Neither the seller nor the lender is likely to make repairs to the property.** Many short sale properties have deferred maintenance, as the seller may stop paying for maintenance as money becomes tight. By the time the sale occurs, many short sale sellers are either unable or unwilling to pay for repairs. They realize that every dollar they spend on the property is a dollar they will not receive back. If a buyer wants to purchase a short sale and the property requires repairs before the buyer's bank will lend any money, the buyer should find a way to make the repairs themselves or find a different property to buy. There is a risk to the buyer repairing a house before they purchase it or obtain a short sale approval to purchase it. If the buyer improves the house and the short sale fails or the buyer opts to walk away, then the buyer will have wasted their time and money on a house they will not own. Furthermore, few contractors will work on a property and wait to be paid at closing.

2. **If the buyer waits until after the short sale approval is granted to ask for a repair concession or lower price, it is far less likely to be approved.** Some buyers wish to wait until after a written short sale approval is granted before they conduct their home inspection. In a regular transaction, the inspection period may be an opportunity for the buyer to request a credit or price reduction for repairs. Buyers should realize that if the seller's lender has already approved a short sale, then it is highly unlikely that the lender will allow a price reduction or repair credit. If a buyer believes that a repair credit or price reduction may be needed, they should conduct their home inspection right after the signing of the real estate contract. It is much easier to amend the price or terms of the

126

transaction before the seller's lender makes a final decision. In most short sale transactions, it is better for the buyer to conduct their home inspection right away instead of waiting for a short sale approval.

3. **It may take months to receive a response from the seller's bank.** Short sales happen gradually, then suddenly. A buyer who must move into a home within 60 days of submitting an offer should seriously consider making an offer on a property that is not a short sale. The closing date is hard to predict early in a short sale negotiation process. Furthermore, there is a risk that a short sale may not be approved, and the buyer may not learn of this until weeks have passed. Anyone who wishes to buy a short sale should be patient and not under pressure to move in soon.

4. **If the buyer is under contract with the seller, take steps to ensure that the seller is committed to the transaction.** The policy on how to mark a short sale listing in the Multiple Listing Service (Pending, Available with Contingency, or Available, among others) is subject to the office's Broker of Record and perhaps the local Association of REALTORS®. Once a seller signs an offer from a buyer, some listing agents mark the listing as being under contract with no more showings as a sign that the seller is committed to that buyer. Other listing agents continue to market the property, soliciting offers that may be superior to the one that the seller already signed. If the listing agent continues to advertise the property, that could jeopardize the initial buyer's position, as there is a distinct possibility that the listing agent and seller may seek to terminate the contract in favor of a better offer. If the buyer has already paid for inspections, an appraisal, an interest rate lock, and other costs associated with the purchase of real estate, the buyer may forfeit those costs if their contract is terminated. In some states, the policy is to have the property remain active or available in the MLS even though the seller is under contract with a buyer. Regardless, the buyer and their agent should convey their high level of commitment to the seller and elicit a high level of commitment in return.

5. **Be prepared to pay a little more at closing, as last-minute payoffs creep up that the seller and their bank may not pay.** As the final fees and costs are tallied on the Settlement Statement, there is a possibility that someone will have to pay more than expected. A water bill that is higher than planned, a late fee added to a delinquent lien, or a property tax credit that is smaller than anticipated could increase the seller's costs.

However, the seller may not have the funds to pay the extra cost, and the bank may be unwilling to take less to cover the shortfall. That may mean the buyer has to pay a little more just to ensure that the transaction occurs. The buyer should be prepared to absorb several hundred dollars in additional costs just in case.

Can We Schedule the Settlement When We Do Not Have the Short Sale Approval from the Lender?

The buyer and buyer agent should refrain from scheduling a firm closing date until short sale approval is granted for all liens *and* the seller expresses that they are satisfied with the approval terms. If the seller receives a short sale approval, it does not automatically mean that they are willing to accept the terms. The buyer should not be taking a day off work, nor packing up the moving truck, nor terminating their lease until they know they are cleared to purchase the property.

If a buyer picks an arbitrary closing date before the short sale has been approved, they are setting themselves up for a costly disappointment. Just because the real estate contract names a date for closing does not mean that the buyer can go ahead and hold settlement on or before that date. We have seen situations where the buyer moved out of their prior residence too early and had to live out of a hotel for many days.

If the seller has two liens that require a short sale, the buyer needs to wait until both liens grant short sale approval. A short sale approval for one lien does not mean that a closing should be scheduled in the hope that the second lien will be approved in time.

I suggest that the buyer and buyer agent stay flexible. They should only schedule a specific date for closing once all approvals are in and the seller consents to the approval terms.

CHAPTER 30. IF I'M UNDER CONTRACT TO BUY A SHORT SALE, CAN I MOVE IN EARLY AND RENT THE HOME?

Those who start with little money are more likely to succeed than those who start with too much. Energy and imagination are the springboards to wealth creation.

- Brian Tracy

The seller's lender often takes a long time to make a decision on a short sale offer, which can wreak havoc with the buyer's plans. Buyers often have to make decisions of their own, such as when to sell their house or terminate their lease, when to enroll their children in the new school district, and when to schedule the movers.

While waiting for a short sale approval on a vacant property, many buyers wonder if they could simply move into the house that they are planning to buy. There are pros and cons to a buyer renting and occupying a home that they have not yet purchased.

Risks to a buyer who rents the home before buying it

- **Insurance.** Some sellers stop paying for homeowner's insurance, and it may take some time for the seller's mortgage lender to step in and pay for insurance. There is the possibility that the property might be uninsured for a time. If the house burns or is damaged in another way, there might not be insurance proceeds to repair the damage. Even if the seller maintains insurance, their standard policy might only provide coverage if the property is owner-occupied.

- **Cost of moving out.** If the short sale is not approved, or if the buyer is unable to purchase property due to financing or title issues, then the buyer will have to pay to move out of the property.

- **Foreclosure notices.** Most short sales involve a borrower who is delinquent on their payments, so the buyer who rents the home may receive visits from Sheriff's deputies or other officers of the court who are delivering foreclosure notices. It may be embarrassing or disruptive for someone to receive notices even though they're not the borrower.

- **Maintenance.** Some sellers might not have the means or the desire to conduct upkeep of the property. Therefore, the property might suffer from deferred maintenance or the buyer will be expected to handle the upkeep.

- **Improvements.** Some buyers, believing that they will definitely buy the home soon, pay for renovations. However, if the sale does not occur, then it is highly unlikely that the buyer will receive compensation for the repairs. If the buyer is forced to move out due to the failure of the house to sell as planned, then the buyer typically forfeits all the money they spent on the renovations.

Risks to a seller who rents the home to the buyer before a sale occurs

- **Liability.** If the home is not properly insured, the owner of record still bears responsibility for whatever occurs on the premises. If the buyer or their guests are injured, the seller is still responsible. If the property is damaged by a fire, a fallen tree, or other event, then the seller may contractually be obligated to pay for repairs.

- **Accusations of misuse of the rent.** The buyer may question what the seller is doing with the rent money if they're not paying the mortgage lender, the insurance policy, or for property maintenance.

- **Maintenance.** The buyer, as a tenant, may expect that the seller perform the duties normally expected of a landlord. The buyer may expect the landlord to conduct maintenance and repairs.

- **Alterations.** Some buyers, believing that they can do with the home as they wish, may knock down walls or make other major alterations to the property. If the buyer conducts demolition or renovation work and later fails to purchase the property, then the seller may be stuck with a house in worse condition than when they gave possession to the buyer.

- **Breach of the lease term.** If the seller signs a long-term lease with the buyer, and the house is foreclosed before the end of the lease, then the seller will have breached the lease by failing to provide housing. Depending on how the lease is written, the seller may be liable for providing housing or compensation to the buyer for failure to uphold the lease for the duration of the term.

- **Assignment of rents.** Some mortgage paperwork gives the lender the right to collect the rent if the borrower defaults. It is possible that the lender may call for an assignment of rents and have the legal right to receive the rent that the seller was counting on.

- **Eviction.** If the buyer does not pay the rent, then the seller may have to initiate foreclosure proceedings.

- **Short sale disapproval.** If the seller receives a substantial amount of rent, their mortgage lender might decline the short sale due to the seller having too much income.

There are other issues surrounding the pre-settlement occupancy of the house by the buyer. One is how much rent the buyer should pay, and how that rent should be allocated. Some buyers might insist upon paying no rent whatsoever, as they may argue that the seller is not going to pay the mortgage lender. Other buyers may request to pay a below-market rent. The amount of rent to be paid is negotiable.

The disbursement of the rent is also negotiable. Generally in a landlord-tenant relationship, the landlord receives all the rent. However, the buyer might ask to place the monthly rent into an escrow account. Some buyers may desire to build up some money in the escrow account to be allocated toward their down payment. Depending upon the escrow agreement between the parties, the buyer might agree to disburse some of the funds to the seller or to repairmen. It is possible that the buyer might seek to have the funds released back to them if the short sale is not approved. Having the buyer move in prior to the sale is a creative solution in some cases, but it is one that also brings potential pitfalls.

CHAPTER 31. REALTOR® SHORT SALE HORROR STORIES

Life's challenges are not supposed to paralyze you, they're supposed to help you discover who you are.

- Bernice Johnson Reagon

The Buyer Had to Pay for a Hotel Room for a Couple of Weeks and Will Never Use Their Agent Again

The closing date in the Agreement of Sale may mean little if the short sale is not yet approved. An agent's buyer insisted upon seeing a home listed as a short sale. Their offer was accepted by the seller and then submitted to the seller's mortgage lender for short sale approval. The representative at the seller's bank told the listing agent over the phone that the short sale would be approved, with the written approval to be faxed within a few days. As soon as he got off the phone with the bank, the listing agent told the buyer's agent right away about the good news. The buyer's agent immediately told the buyer and their title agent that the short sale had been approved. The buyer terminated their lease and scheduled a date for the closing.

Unfortunately, the seller's bank reassigned the loan negotiator before he could issue the written approval, so it was never faxed. Unbeknownst to everyone else in the transaction, the seller's bank neglected the file. On the day before the scheduled closing, the title agent asked the listing agent for the written short sale approval. The listing agent had never received it from the seller's lender. When the listing agent tried to call the representative he had been dealing with, he was sent to other people at the bank who did not know what file he was talking about.

The buyer, believing that the closing was going to happen the next day, decided to stay at a hotel for the night and parked their fully-loaded moving truck in the parking lot. However, without the written short sale approval, the title company would not hold settlement. The buyer decided to stay another night at the hotel, thinking that settlement would occur the next day.

Two weeks later, the seller's bank still had not responded to the repeated requests for a written short sale approval. The buyer had to place all their items in a storage facility and had exhausted their short-term savings on hotel costs. The buyer voiced their dissatisfaction with their agent, who passed blame on to the listing agent and the seller's bank.

After another two weeks, the buyer had moved into a relative's house temporarily while they waited for settlement. Finally, a supervisor at the seller's bank authorized the short sale in writing, and the settlement occurred. The buyer angrily told their agent they wanted some compensation for all the time and money they had spent waiting for the closing. The seller did not have any money to give, and the seller's bank refused to offer any concessions. The buyers decided to go ahead with the settlement, but they were so upset they refused to speak with their agent again.

The REALTOR® Was Sued for Successfully Processing the Short Sale

The listing agent did exactly what he promised his sellers he would do. He listed their short sale property. He procured a buyer. The agent negotiated with the sellers' bank and convinced them to approve the short sale. At the settlement, the sellers cried tears of joy and gratitude, thanking the agent profusely for selling their house.

Thirty days after the sale of the house, the former owners received notice of a lawsuit from their mortgage lender. The bank filed a lawsuit for the entire remaining balance of the mortgage. The former owners thought there must have been some mistake. But there was no mistake, as the bank's attorney pointed out that the mortgage lender stated in the short sale approval letter that they reserved the right to sue for the deficiency. The former owners had never seen the approval letter before, as their real estate agent had handled all the paperwork.

> TAI TIDBITS...
>
> Do not schedule the exact settlement date until you have the written short sale approval letter from the seller's bank.

The bank was awarded a judgment against the former owners for the entire remaining balance, plus collection costs and legal fees. The former owners then sued the agent, his broker, and the brokerage firm for failing to inform them about the bank's decision not to waive the deficiency. They stated that had they known about the bank's intention to pursue a deficiency judgment, they might have renegotiated with the bank or tried an alternative to the short sale. The amount the former owners decided to seek was the entire judgment levied against them, plus their legal fees.

The agent's Errors and Omissions insurance company stated that they would not cover the claim, as short sale negotiation falls outside the normal activities of a real estate agent. The agent and his broker were left to defend themselves without insurance coverage. They eventually had to settle out of court, paying a large sum to dismiss the lawsuit against them.

CHAPTER 32. I WANT TO GIVE MY PROPERTY TO THE BANK. CAN I DO THAT?

In the subprime mortgage industry, bankers handed out iffy loans like candy at a parade because such loans meant revenue and, hence, bonuses for executives in the here-and-now.

- Thomas Frank

Some distressed homeowners have the option to give their property to the bank in a process known as a deed-in-lieu of foreclosure. This is known as a "friendly foreclosure." The homeowner voluntarily conveys clear property title to the lender in exchange for the discharge of the debt.

A lender might consider a deed-in-lieu of foreclosure if the following occurs:

- The lender determines that the borrower faces an involuntary hardship that creates a long-term inability to pay.
- The borrower is cooperative by communicating with the lender and allowing complete access to the property for the lender's inspection and appraisal.
- The borrower is delinquent or faces default.
- The lender sees that the homeowner made a good faith effort to sell the property but was unable to do so.
- There are no other liens or encumbrances against the property.

Sometimes a deed-in-lieu of foreclosure is known as "jingle mail," as the borrower mails the keys to the bank.

One of the risks of a deed-in-lieu of foreclosure is that the borrower has to be careful to ensure that the lender agrees to forgive the remaining debt. Pennsylvania law allows a mortgage lender to initiate a lawsuit within six months after the transfer of a property to recoup the remaining debt. If the lawsuit is initiated within that time, the lender may have up to 20 years to collect on the deficiency judgment.

Many lenders do offer complete debt forgiveness on a deed-in-lieu of foreclosure. However, some banks may keep their options open. If you are considering a deed-in-lieu of foreclosure, then you should hire an attorney to represent your interests.

If a real estate agent has a property listed for sale, then they earn nothing if the owner conveys the property to the bank. In some rare cases, the agent may be able to convince the bank to list the property with them later on when the bank is ready to sell. However, in almost all cases, the lender has a separate department that handles the sale of real estate. That department also has pre-existing relationships with other real estate agents.

If a homeowner wants to give their property to the bank but has signed an Agreement of Sale with a buyer, the seller may not be in a position to terminate the contract without consequences. If you are under contract and wish to pursue a deed-in-lieu of foreclosure, talk with your agent and consult with your attorney.

Some lenders, and some short sale programs, require that the homeowner list their house for a minimum period of time before being considered for a deed-in-lieu of foreclosure. Keep in mind that the banks are not in the business of owning real estate. The lenders are in the business of lending money, so a short sale may be a preferred alternative since the bank never has to take ownership of the property.

As mentioned, a deed-in-lieu of foreclosure will only work if there are no other liens or encumbrances against the property. A mortgage lender will not take the property back if there is a second mortgage or a judgment that must be paid too. If the homeowner has enough money to pay off the secondary liens in full, then a deed-in-lieu of foreclosure becomes more likely. However, one should be careful with paying off secondary liens. It is possible that one could spend a lot of money paying off other liens only to find out that the first mortgage lender decides not to move forward with a deed-in-lieu of foreclosure.

In some circumstances, a homeowner could receive an incentive payment from the lender for a deed-in-lieu of foreclosure. The payment may be for $1,000 or more. That is something that can be negotiated with certain lenders.

In term of damage to credit, a deed-in-lieu of foreclosure is typically the same as a short sale in that the loan is marked as "Paid in full but not as agreed," or "Paid as settled." Another factor to one's credit is whether the loan was delinquent by 30 days or more, as that incurs a separate hit to one's credit score. Other factors affecting one's credit are how many lines of credit are delinquent, the length of time of the delinquency, and the amount of debt.

Allowing the property to simply be foreclosed is more damaging in most situations than a short sale or deed-in-lieu of foreclosure. In most cases, it is best not to walk away. An alternative to foreclosure should always be considered.

CHAPTER 33. WHAT ARE THE LAWS GOVERNING THE SHORT SALE INDUSTRY?

And once the storm is over, you won't remember how you made it through, how you managed to survive. You won't even be sure, whether the storm is really over. But one thing is certain. When you come out of the storm, you won't be the same person who walked in. That's what this storm's all about.

- Haruki Murakami

The Mortgage Assistance Relief Services (MARS) Rule

In late 2010, the Federal Trade Commission (FTC) issued a rule to protect struggling homeowners from mortgage relief scams. Hundreds of thousands of distressed borrowers had been scammed out of hundreds of millions of dollars by peddlers of mortgage relief services that were either outright scams or were completely ineffective at delivering results.

The MARS Rule includes the following protections for homeowners:

- *Ban on advance fees*. The most significant consumer protection under the MARS Rule is that no mortgage relief company may collect any fee until they have provided the borrower with a written offer from their lender that the borrower decides is acceptable. Furthermore, the company must also remind the borrower of their right to reject the offer without any fee being charged. In other words, the homeowner cannot be charged a fee by the mortgage relief service until there is an acceptable loan modification or short sale approval.

- *Disclosures*. The Rule mandates that mortgage relief companies must disclose information to homeowners to protect them from being misled. The companies must reveal in their advertising toward individual borrowers that:

  - The company is not associated with the government, and their services have not been approved by the government or the mortgage lender,

  - The lender may not agree to change the consumer's loan,

- If the borrower stops paying their mortgage, they could lose their home and damage their credit.

- *Ability to cancel at any time.* Companies must explain in their communications that the borrower can stop doing business with them at any time. The borrower can accept or reject any offer of mortgage assistance obtained from the lender, and if the borrower rejects it, they do not have to pay the company's fee. The amount of the fee must also be disclosed.

- *Prohibited claims.* The MARS Rule prohibits mortgage relief companies from making false or misleading claims, including claims about:

  - The cost of the service,

  - The company's affiliation with the government or other institutions,

  - The company's refund and cancellation policy,

  - Whether the company has actually performed the service it promised,

  - Whether the company will provide legal representation to the borrower,

  - The availability or cost of any alternative mortgage relief service,

  - The amount of time the borrower will save by using the company,

  - The borrower's payment and other mortgage obligations, and/or

  - The likelihood of the borrower achieving the result they desire.

- *Communication with the lender or servicer.* Mortgage relief services cannot tell borrowers to stop communicating with their lender.

Attorneys are generally exempt from the MARS Rule if they meet the following conditions:

- They are licensed in the state where the homeowner or the property is located,

- They are complying with state laws, and

- To be exempt from the advance fee ban, attorneys must place any fees they collect in a client trust account and abide by state laws covering that account.

Real estate brokers and agents are exempt from certain provisions of the MARS Rule. The disclosure provisions of the MARS Rule will not be enforced against agents who:

- Are licensed and in good standing with their state,

- Comply with state laws governing the practice of real estate licensees, and

- Assist or attempt to assist homeowners in obtaining short sales in the course of working to sell their houses.

Therefore, agents do not have to make any of the disclosures and they may collect advance fees in the form of a real estate commission. Agents must, however, comply with the Rule's ban on misrepresentations. Agents who attempt to negotiate loan modifications must still adhere to the Rule since that form of mortgage relief is not related to the sale of real estate.

While the MARS Rule was instituted by the FTC, it is now under the jurisdiction of the newly formed Consumer Finance Protection Bureau (CFPB). Their website is www.consumerfinance.gov.

Legal Issues with Short Sales

We've described many of the benefits of a successful short sale. Now we're going to make you aware of many of the legal problems associated with short sales.

Consequences for Agents

- *Inability to Handle the Workload.* Some real estate agents, in order to obtain a listing, promise their clients that they'll personally process the short sale. There are numerous situations where the agent becomes overwhelmed and fails to follow up on case files. In short sales, time is of the essence. Sellers face a foreclosure date that may be difficult to delay. If the agent fails to process the short sale in a timely manner, the seller could lose the property to foreclosure. In some cases, sellers have initiated lawsuits against inexperienced or overwhelmed agents for bungling the short sale negotiation.

- *Misrepresenting Tax Consequences.* Sometimes a person inexperienced with short sales may inform borrowers that they will not face any taxation on forgiven mortgage debt. Historically, the Internal Revenue Service (IRS) has treated cancelled or forgiven debt as if it were income, which means that a person has to pay income tax on the forgiven amount. Some taxpayers will not have to pay any income tax on debt forgiven via a short sale. The Mortgage Forgiveness Debt Relief Act of 2007 applies to certain mortgage debts forgiven in years 2007 through 2016. The Act generally allows taxpayers to exclude income from the discharge of debt on their principal residence. Debt reduced to mortgage restructuring and mortgage debt forgiven in connection with a foreclosure action both qualify for relief. Up to $2 million of forgiven mortgage debt (if married, filing jointly) qualifies for the tax relief. Up to $1 million of forgiven debt is permitted for taxpayers who file individually. Debt used to refinance a primary residence qualifies for the tax relief, but only up to the amount of the old mortgage immediately before the refinancing. It is important for a seller to consult with their accountant, tax preparer, or tax attorney to see if they will qualify for tax relief.

- *Leading the Seller to Believe That All Their Debt is Forgiven.* A seller may believe that they can walk away from the short sale with no further liability to pay off debt. In many cases that is true, but in other cases the lender may pursue the seller for the remaining balance. Holders of second mortgages or deeds of trust sometimes do not forgive the debt. In some short sales, the second mortgage holder accepts a partial payment to release the mortgage lien, but they later sell the balance to a collection agency. Also, it is imperative for the agent and seller to understand whether they have a recourse or non-recourse loan. With a recourse loan, unless otherwise stated in the short sale approval paperwork, the lender may later seek payment of the remaining debt. An irate seller who finds out a year later that they still owe money might sue the agent who handled the short sale. It is best to have the seller review the short sale approval document with their attorney to determine if there would be any continued debt obligation after the short sale. Our short sale program provides an attorney to represent the seller if they do not have one. That attorney will review the short sale approval letter with the seller and advise them whether to accept the terms and conditions. Find out more at www.shortsalebook.com.

- *Failing to Uphold One's Fiduciary Duty.* A real estate licensee has a fiduciary duty to do what is best for the client. If a listing agent allows a "double-close and flip" scenario, the seller client may feel that the agent failed to bring the highest and best offer. The situation will be compounded if the seller client must pay income taxes on a larger portion of forgiven debt than they would have.

Some Opportunists and Investors May Induce the Seller and Agent to Commit Mortgage Fraud

When a short sale is listed, some sellers and agents are besieged by unorthodox requests from seemingly helpful real estate investors or other short sale opportunists. Of course many buyers look for a good deal, and it is the bank's prerogative to allow a property to be sold for less than fair market value. However, some of these investors or opportunists may entangle the agent and seller in what amounts to mortgage fraud.

One fraudulent situation is the double-close-and-flip transaction. That occurs when an investor places the property under contract at a low price and offers to negotiate that offer with the bank. Meanwhile, the investor tells the listing agent to continue marketing the property so they can procure a much higher offer. The investor tells the bank that the low offer is the only one, while concealing the much higher offer from the bank. The investor's intention is to engineer the transaction so they can collect the difference between the low offer and the higher offer while keeping the bank unaware. The listing agent, who has a fiduciary duty to the seller, ends up procuring a higher offer for the investor's benefit and not the seller's benefit. Furthermore, the short sale fraud department within many banks may sue all the parties if they discover that a double-close-and-flip transaction occurred.

For example, the investor may go under contract with the seller at a sale price of $100,000. The investor tells the listing agent that they will receive six percent commission, which is $6,000. The investor tells the seller's lender that $100,000 is the only offer received. The investor may even have the seller sign the deed over to them, or the investor might file an option on the public records. The deed and the option each give the investor incredible control over the transaction, and it is hard to push the investor out of the deal later. So, while the investor is negotiating a $100,000 sale with the mortgage lender, the investor tells the listing agent to keep marketing the property. The agent procures an offer for $135,000. The investor instructs the buyer to give them $35,000 and says the buyer can take over their contract to buy the property for $100,000. Or the investor convinces the buyer to give them the $135,000, and the investor uses $100,000 of that money to buy the house and even pays the agent another commission on the $135,000 sale. Then the investor signs a deed immediately thereafter, transferring ownership to the end buyer while pocketing the difference. The fraud occurs in the misrepresentation to the bank, who may later claim that they were defrauded of out tens of thousands of dollars. That is the equivalent of walking into a bank branch and robbing the teller of tens of thousands of dollars. The agent and seller may be found to be complicit in the fraud, even if they were somewhat naïve to the investor's intentions.

Another potentially fraudulent situation involves the investor placing an option on the property or inducing the seller to turn over the deed without paying off the mortgage. The investor creates a cloud on the title and then demands a payment from the ultimate buyer to release their option or transfer the deed.

The third type of fraudulent transaction involves a non-arms-length transaction or collusion in which the buyer allows the seller to remain in the property. Some sellers convince a family member, often with a different last name, to buy the house at a discount. Then the family member either rents or sells the house back to the former borrower. The bank is defrauded out of thousands of dollars.

Some Sellers May Attempt to Defraud Their Bank

In some situations, it is the seller who attempts to defraud their lender by encouraging their agent to allow a family member or business associate to surreptitiously purchase the house. The intent of the seller is to have their family member or associate pretend to be someone they do not know, and then the bank may allow the house to be sold for a discount along with the debt being forgiven. That way the seller receives the benefit of staying in the house while being relieved of the debt obligation. Some sellers may believe that if their family member or associate has a different last name, then the lender will believe it is an arms-length transaction. If a lender discovers that the sale was not an arms-length transaction, they have the right to file criminal charges and initiate a civil lawsuit against all the parties involved.

CHAPTER 34. WHAT ARE THE TRENDS IN THE SHORT SALE INDUSTRY?

But that's the challenge – to change the system more than it changes you.

- Michael Pollan

How Short Sales Have Changed Recently, and How It Affects You

Banks and servicers were designed to collect mortgage payments or foreclose. When the housing crisis hit in 2008, these institutions were not equipped to handle the deluge of borrower requests for loan modifications, forbearance plans, short sales, sale-leaseback plans, and deed-in-lieu of foreclosure transfers. Prior to the crisis, lenders could simply foreclose and recoup their investment because of the ever-increasing housing values.

The banks and servicers offered few alternatives to foreclosure, lost paperwork, took months or years to approve short sales, and even foreclosed on borrowers after offering them alternatives to foreclosure. There were even stories about lenders who foreclosed on homes that had no mortgages.

One glaring problem for struggling homeowners was that almost all the lenders had a policy whereby they would only consider someone for a short sale if they were delinquent on their payments. Many homeowners were trying to do the responsible thing by paying their mortgage and sacrificing on other expenditures. Many people who needed a short sale to sell their house ended up not even being considered for one. People were faced with the decision of deliberately defaulting on their mortgage just to be considered for a short sale. The policies of the lenders seemed bizarre and illogical to many struggling borrowers.

Another problem for people seeking a short sale was that the lenders would only make a decision on whether to approve a short sale if there was an offer from a buyer. The lender would give no communication or suggestion prior to the submission of an offer on what might be considered acceptable. Real estate agents and sellers were not sure of what list price to use. Once an offer would finally come in, the lenders would take so long to make a decision that the buyer would walk away, thus wasting many months of effort. Real estate agents and sellers would ask the lenders to provide some guidance on what would be an acceptable price. Yet in the past, banks would typically not grant a short sale pre-approval.

A major challenge for the banks (that they helped to create) was that many struggling homeowners decided to stop paying their mortgage and live in the house rent-free for as long as possible. Since the banks were offering no real solutions and since they were taking so long to consider a short sale, frustrated borrowers made a pragmatic choice to save up their money while living for free in their own home. Some people were able to stay for a few years before being foreclosed. While some borrowers felt they had no other choice, others derived some satisfaction in sticking it to the banks.

Another challenge for the banks (that they helped to create) was that many real estate agents did not want to work on short sales, particularly because the lenders were cutting commission. Real estate agents know that short sales involve more work and more risk because of the high probability of not selling the property. Lenders were exacerbating the problem because they were cutting commissions. So agents were doing more work, with more risk, for ultimately less money. Without the cooperation of agents, many short sales failed or never reached the settlement table. Lenders needed to find a way to incentivize agents, or at the very least, avoid demoralizing the professionals who make sales happen.

In the past few years, many lenders and servicers have shifted toward offering viable alternatives to foreclosure. These alternatives include:

- FHA and Fannie Mae reduced the waiting period for people to qualify for a mortgage after a recent bankruptcy, pre-foreclosure, or short sale. FHA introduced a Back to Work program that cuts the mandatory waiting period down to just one year after a significant derogatory event. Fannie Mae cut their waiting period down to two years. A significant derogatory event includes a pre-foreclosure, a short sale, a deed-in-lieu of foreclosure, a bankruptcy, and a mortgage charge-off.

- Bank of America offered a program to several thousand borrowers to deed their house back to the bank, and the bank would allow them to rent the house.

- Many servicers offered to streamline their short sale evaluation process to increase the time it takes to grant an approval.

146

- Fannie Mae and Freddie Mac unveiled a new, standardized short sale program on November 1, 2012 that will allow people who are current on their payments to be considered for a short sale. The program also pays $3,000 to short sale sellers at the settlement. It allows military service members on active duty to receive consideration for a short sale when they change duty stations. The program also promises a 30-60 day response if a signed real estate contract is submitted, provided that the seller has turned in all the paperwork requested.

- Some lenders offered a relocation incentive to help the seller move after a short sale. These payments generally is $3,000, while at the height of the short sale crisis some payments ranged from $10,000 to $45,000.

- Some banks, like Bank of America, started offering principal extinguishment on secondary liens. They mailed letters to selected borrowers who were delinquent, stating that the entire debt on the second mortgage was forgiven. In short sales, essentially the secondary lien holders receive nothing because there is absolutely no equity nor are housing values expected to rise enough in the near future. Collection efforts were futile, so in many cases it makes sense to simply write off the entire loan.

- Some lenders are proactively offering cash-for-keys, which essentially means that the delinquent borrower gives the deed and the house keys to the lender in exchange for a check. The typical payment may be around $2,000 to $3,000. In some cases, the lender offers to forgive the remaining debt and part ways with the borrower.

- Many lenders are now offering short sale pre-approvals under certain programs. They are evaluating people for short sales even when there is no offer on the table. They are sometimes telling agents and sellers what price they would accept.

- Some lenders are offering a particular customer service representative to help a particular borrower. Instead of a seller and their agent talking to a different person at the bank every time they call, some lenders are assigning a specific individual. That increases the likelihood of a successful sale.

- Bank of America started hiring third party companies to represent them and attempt to negotiate a short sale or deed-in-lieu of foreclosure with delinquent borrowers. These subcontractors work for the bank and can often move more quickly than the bank could. Also, some borrowers are so frustrated with their bank that a third party can reduce the potential for confrontation and increase the possibility of collaboration.

- Lenders have improved their short sale software and online interfaces with agents and sellers. More lenders now use the www.Equator.com interface, which encourages communication and helps to hold banks more accountable. Other banks have developed their own software or systems, which increase efficiency.

The actions of the lenders, servicers, and entities like Fannie Mae and Freddie Mac indicate a shift away from foreclosure and toward other alternatives, particularly the short sale. The banks now realize that in most cases, a short sale produces more money for the bank than a foreclosure. The banks do not have the ability to handle property management and the responsibilities of owning houses. It is better for the lenders to help the borrower avoid foreclosure. Foreclosure also hurts the community and taxpayers.

In the coming year, it is expected that there will be fewer short sale listings than before. I believe there will be a higher probability of those short sales actually reaching settlement. Lenders are steadily reducing the roadblocks that cause delays and failed closings. Agents and homebuyers are given more certainty and confidence that transactions will work out in the end. Sellers are given more options and more responsiveness from the lenders.

It is also expected that some short sale sellers will have to submit less paperwork than in the past. Lenders may make faster decisions with less information.

More and more people who are current on their mortgage but still struggling financially will be considered for short sales. Many Americans have a few months' worth of savings, yet they need to sell their house and cannot make up the shortfall on the mortgage. So a short sale is their best option. Fewer people have to deliberately stop paying their mortgage to be considered for a short sale. This change will produce a deluge of short sale listings, as the pool of potential short sale sellers has increased in size.

The short sale industry has more third party companies and law firms that specialize in short sale negotiation on behalf of sellers. Streamlined procedures and high levels of experience at these firms benefit sellers, as they are more likely to be well represented and reach a successful conclusion. Expect to see a small handful of third party companies and law firms capture a large portion of the market as they increase their ability to help struggling homeowners.

For someone considering a short sale or other alternative to foreclosure, now is the best time ever to move forward with one of those options. The industry is changing, and more help is available.

What is a Bank Walkaway?

A bank walkaway is a situation where the mortgage lender decides to charge off a defaulted loan and cancel a foreclosure action. The lender might do this if they deem that it would cost more money to foreclose and take back the property.

This bank walkaway phenomenon began in earnest in 2009. Detroit and Chicago are the cities with the most bank walkaways.

Below are several bank walkaway scenarios.

1. The lender begins the foreclosure process, the occupants move out, and the lender later decides to cancel the foreclosure action. The owner assumes that the foreclosure sale occurred. Many months or years later, after the house has been vandalized and loses tremendous value, the city informs the owner that they are responsible for the property.

2. The lender decides not to begin foreclosure proceedings. The lender may sell the defaulted note to a collection agency or another bank for pennies on the dollar. Eventually, the collection agency or bank may charge off the loan but not release the lien.

3. The borrower declares bankruptcy, but the lender never files a Proof of Claim or moves to lift the automatic stay. The lien typically remains, but the lender stops trying to collect payments on the loan.

4. In what is known as principal extinguishment, the lender agrees to charge off the debt and satisfy the mortgage lien. This is the best scenario for the borrower if their desire is to keep the property.

What is Principal Extinguishment?

Principal extinguishment is a growing trend among mortgage lenders, particularly secondary lienholders. Principal extinguishment is a negotiated agreement between the lender and the borrower whereby the lender agrees to release all of the remaining debt and satisfy the mortgage lien. In other words, the lender tells the borrower that they no longer owe any money and the lien will be removed.

The borrower will likely receive a 1099-C from the lender for the amount of the forgiven debt. The borrower may have to pay tax to the Internal Revenue Service (IRS) on the forgiven debt.

Principal extinguishment is slightly different than principal reduction. Principal reduction involves the removal of some of the underlying debt, but the borrower will still be responsible for the remaining debt. The mortgage lien will not be satisfied until the balance of the loan is paid in full.

Since We're Negotiating a Loan Modification or Short Sale, Does that Mean the Bank Will Stop Their Foreclosure Action Against Us?

In many cases, a mortgage lender will continue the foreclosure action even though they are negotiating a loan modification or short sale with the borrower. Just because someone is working on a loan modification or short sale does not mean that the bank halts the foreclosure proceeding.

The perspective of the lender is that if the loan modification or short sale fails, then they can quickly finalize the foreclosure. We have also seen situations where the bank negotiator states that they will temporarily stop the foreclosure action, but the borrower receives notice of an impending foreclosure sale. Those are frequently cases of the left hand not knowing what the right hand is doing at the bank.

In some loan modification and short sale programs, the lender agrees to stop the foreclosure action for the duration of the program. For example, the foreclosure action is halted on FHA loans that are granted a short sale pre-approval, known as an Approval to Participate (ATP). If the house does not sell during the listing period, then the borrower may transfer ownership via a deed-in-lieu of foreclosure and they will not be liable for any deficiency amount.

It's the End of Dual-Tracking as We Know It, and I Feel Fine.

The Consumer Financial Protection Bureau (CFPB) introduced new rules that became effective in January 2014. Dual-tracking is a situation where a mortgage

150

lender continues a foreclosure action against a delinquent borrower while simultaneously working with the borrower to avoid foreclosure. The new rules originated from the Dodd-Frank Wall Street Reform and Consumer Protection Act.

The problem with dual-tracking for borrowers is that many people were foreclosed upon even though their lender told them they were being considered for a loan modification, short sale, or deed-in-lieu of foreclosure. We have seen situations where a homeowner was told that their short sale was verbally approved and that a written approval was coming in the next few days. However, the bank foreclosed on them shortly thereafter, having never issued a written approval as promised. The lender's negotiators typically take no responsibility whatsoever, claiming that they could not convince their own employer to stop the foreclosure action.

Lenders preferred to engage in dual-tracking because they could quickly foreclose on a borrower if the loan modification, forbearance, short sale, or deed-in-lieu process failed or if the process was taking too long. However, in many instances the process was taking so long because of the lender's bureaucracy, high staff turnover, and ever-changing policies. So, the lender created the very situation that caused them to fail to make a decision on whether to approve an alternative to foreclosure.

The CFPB rules do not prohibit dual-tracking entirely. The rules do impose some limits. The main stipulations are:

- A lender cannot initiate a foreclosure until 120 days after a borrower falls delinquent.

- A lender cannot start a foreclosure if a borrower has a pending application for a loan modification.

- A lender must give borrowers who are two months behind written notice of alternatives to foreclosure and examples of those options.

- A lender must provide delinquent borrowers with direct, easy, ongoing access to staff responsible for helping them with their application and reporting the status of an application.

- If a borrower asks for a loan modification after the 120-day delinquency period, the lender may continue the foreclosure process.

- A servicer must offer all foreclosure alternatives available from the investor or loan owner, and not just the option that is most financially favorable to the servicer.

- Before interest rates adjust, lenders must provide clear mortgage statements with warnings about the upcoming adjustment.

- Lenders must consider and respond to a borrower's application for a loan modification if it arrives at least 37 days before a scheduled foreclosure sale. If the lender offers an alternative to foreclosure, they must give the borrower time to accept the offer before pushing for a foreclosure judgment or a foreclosure sale. Lenders may not foreclose on a property if the borrower and the lender have agreed to a loss mitigation agreement, as long as the borrower abides by that agreement.

- Banks that service 5,000 or fewer loans are exempt from certain requirements.

- Lenders must provide to the borrower advance notice and pricing on force-place insurance if the lender has reason to believe that the property is no longer insured by the borrower.

CHAPTER 35. THE RIGHT MINDSET TO DEAL WITH A SHORT SALE

When faced with a challenge, happy families, like happy people, just add a new chapter to their life story that shows them overcoming the hardship. This skill is particularly important for children, whose identity tends to get locked in during adolescence.

- Bruce Feiler

Short Sales Are Simple, but Not Easy.

Short sales are simple, but not easy. Short sales in real estate are fairly straightforward, and follow these steps:

1. The seller owes more than the property is worth and has a compelling reason to sell.

2. The seller submits paperwork to their mortgage lender to justify their inability to pay.

3. The property is listed for sale by a real estate agent at a price at or slightly below fair market value.

4. A ready, willing, and able buyer submits an offer.

5. The seller accepts the offer.

6. The Agreement of Sale is submitted to the seller's lender for a short sale approval or denial.

7. The lender sends either an appraiser or an agent to the property to provide an opinion of value.

8. If the valuation is close enough to the sale price in the Agreement of Sale, a short sale approval is issued in writing.

9. If the seller agrees to the short sale approval conditions, then everyone prepares for the settlement.

153

10. The lender reviews the final HUD-1 Settlement Statement shortly before closing, and if it meets their criteria the sale goes forward as planned.

So the steps are easy to understand. Yet the process is far from easy. Short sales involve numerous moving parts that must align or the transaction is unlikely to occur.

If the sale price in the Agreement of Sale is too low relative to the lender's valuation, the short sale will not be approved. If the bank's valuation is too high, then no buyer will pay enough to meet the lender's desired amount. If the property is listed too high by the agent, then buyers may not be interested enough to make an offer. If the seller does not submit the paperwork the lender requires, then the short sale will not be approved.

If the buyer becomes impatient and backs out of the deal, then the transaction is unlikely to happen. If the foreclosure sale date is in the near future, the bank may simply allow the property to be sold at the foreclosure auction. If the lender's staff is overwhelmed or inexperienced, they may prevent the short sale from being approved.

If the seller owes other creditors with liens on the property, those creditors might prevent the sale. If the lender has strict deadlines for submission of documents and a deadline is missed, that can prevent a short sale from being approved. If the property is damaged from vandals, frozen pipes, or other calamities, the seller might not have the funds or the ability to make repairs.

For a short sale to work, all the parties in the transaction must be patient and flexible. Remember, the process is simple, but not easy.

Know Who Is on Your Team, and Then Work Closely with Your Teammates.

In a traditional, non-distressed transaction, generally it is the buyer versus the seller. The buyer wants to purchase at a lower price and with terms favorable to them. The seller wants to sell at a higher price with terms advantageous to them. If there are real estate agents or lawyers involved, the agents and lawyers are there to guide and advise their client to do what is in their best interests. In many cases, it is better for the buyer and seller not to interact directly but via their agents or attorneys. Therefore, if one looked at the transaction as a sporting contest, it would be the buyer's team versus the seller's team.

In a short sale transaction, the teams are the seller's lender versus everyone else. In other words, it is the mortgage company versus the seller, buyer, seller's agent, buyer's agent, seller's attorney, and buyer's attorney. Successful short sale transactions often require the buyer and seller to work in a more collaborative fashion than in a traditional real estate sale.

The buyer might have to do things that normally the seller does. For example, a seller was so destitute that they could not afford to continue paying for heat in the winter. The seller could have easily shut off the utilities and hoped that the pipes would not freeze and burst. The buyer, however, needed the utilities to stay on so they could conduct their home inspection and because their bank's appraiser required that the utilities be on for their appraisal visit. In a collaborative fashion, the seller stated their need to save money and the buyer stated their need to have the utilities activated. Even though the Agreement of Sale stated that the seller must keep the utilities on, and even though in a traditional transaction the buyer does not take over the utilities until the sale date, the buyer agreed to take over the utilities a few weeks before the closing. Therefore, the seller and buyer worked together to solve a problem.

Focus on the Outcome, Not so Much the Process.

Short sales are inherently uncertain transactions. The parties do not know if and when the seller's lender will approve the short sale. For a long time, the parties do not know what the lender's approved sale price will be, they do not know when the settlement date will occur, and they do not know if they will have to contribute more money to make the sale happen.

A lot of finger-pointing and stress can occur in a short sale transaction. Emotions can become heated. A seller may be so embarrassed or frustrated with the condition of their meager finances. They may feel that they have failed. A buyer may be under strain to establish themselves in their home by a certain date. A buyer may be concerned about transferring their kids to a new school district, or changing jobs, or terminating their lease, or locking in a low interest rate, or scheduling days off to handle the move into their new home.

Almost all stress in life is caused by making things out to be bigger than they really are. It is human to blow things out of proportion or assume that others are doing things *to* us instead of *for* us. Usually when we are upset, it is because we perceive that someone else has violated our rules. Yet, we often do not communicate our rules to others, and sometimes we change our rules to fit certain situations. And it is hard for us sometimes to understand that other people have different rules.

For example, a buyer's agent lashed out at a listing agent because the sellers shut off the heat in a vacant house during the winter and the buyers were panicked about the house freezing. The buyer agent's rules were that the seller had to keep the heat on at all costs. The buyer's agent pointed to the real estate contract that was signed between the parties. The listing agent told the sellers about the buyer's concern about damage from freezing pipes. The seller responded angrily that they were so poor that they could either pay to heat a vacant house or feed their children. The seller stated that they had to make a choice to feed their kids with what little money they had. The seller stated that they did not really care what the real estate contract said. Each party applied different sets of rules. What is interesting is that neither party wanted to harm the other. The buyer did not want the seller's children to starve. The seller did not want the pipes to freeze. *People tend to do the best they can with the resources they have available at the moment.*

Many times people create stress for others by focusing more on the process instead of the outcome. The process includes a mismatch of rules, policies, expectations, and emotions. If people focus more on the outcome, then the process becomes much easier to deal with. A person can reduce their stress by having fewer rules. With fewer rules, we open the door to have more understanding of the behavior of others. Also, by having fewer rules, there are fewer opportunities for people to violate our rules.

To reach the desired outcome, which is a short sale settlement that is satisfactory to the buyer and seller, the parties need to be flexible. The parties should eliminate blame from their vocabulary and work together. All blame is disempowering. Blaming other people, or events, or ourselves, does not solve problems. Therefore, blame is useless and serves no purpose. By being flexible, achieving the desired outcome becomes more likely.

CHAPTER 36. NOW THAT I SOLD MY PROPERTY, WHAT CAN I EXPECT?

The most beautiful people I've known are those who have known trials, have known struggles, have known loss, and have found their way out of the depths.

- Elisabeth Kubler-Ross

Because My Credit Score Went Down, I'm Afraid No Landlord Will Rent to Me and My Family. What Do I Do?

The overwhelming number of short sale sellers need to rent a home after they sell their house. Many short sale sellers are concerned that prospective landlords will reject their application to rent based upon a low credit score. Most short sale sellers defaulted on their mortgage loan, so their credit report displays a major delinquency. A fear of some people is that no one will rent to them.

I have found that many landlords are willing to rent to people who just went through a short sale or foreclosure. For some of my past short sale clients, I wrote a letter on their behalf that they included with their application to rent. The foreclosure epidemic affects many people in Pennsylvania, even some landlords. They are likely to understand, and they may even be happy to help someone who is getting over a tough time in their life.

It is best to be open and honest when applying for a rental property after a short sale or foreclosure. You can mention the number of years in which you made timely payments on the mortgage. You can also mention the hardship that occurred which caused the delinquency. You can state that the financial hardship is over and that you now have a steady income once again. You might find that a landlord is interested in renting to you even if your credit score has blemishes.

Will the Bank Send Me a 1099 Form?

Expect your lender to mail you an IRS Form 1099-C after a short sale in which debt was forgiven. It is usually mailed in the January following the sale of the property.

Some short sale sellers attempt to ask their lender not to mail them a 1099. Doing that is futile, as the 1099 is a means for the lender to write off the bad debt. Therefore, expect to receive a 1099 form.

Consult with your tax preparer on how to file your taxes with the IRS. There may be a way to offset the debt forgiveness with other losses or expenses. If you sell your primary residence via a short sale before the end of 2016, you will not owe any taxes on the forgiven debt as long as you include IRS Form 982 with your tax filing.

Should I Hire a Credit Restoration Service?

I recommend that people who have gone through a short sale, a deed-in-lieu of foreclosure, or a foreclosure hire a reputable credit restoration service. A credit restoration service can help improve your credit score faster. They might even be able to expunge negative items from your credit record. It may be best to hire a service that charges a one-time fee versus a monthly fee, as a firm that charges you monthly may not want to work quickly on your behalf.

EPILOGUE

If you could kick the person in the pants responsible for most of your trouble, you wouldn't sit for a month.

- Theodore Roosevelt

When did I first hear about a real estate short sale? It was early March of 2005 when I was at a real estate investing seminar in Valley Forge, Pennsylvania. There were a number of speakers in different rooms. Not knowing what a short sale was, I sat down to listen to the speaker who was touting a short sale educational product he had created. He was scheduled to speak for two hours. I got up after 10 minutes and said to myself, "This is stupid." And I walked out.

In May of 2005 I was introduced to a real estate investor who negotiated a handful of short sales so he could buy those properties at a low price. Within a couple of weeks after meeting, we purchased a short sale together in Lehighton, Pennsylvania. We fixed it ourselves and sold it for a modest profit a few months later. Then we purchased another short sale and did the same thing.

In the fall of 2005, we created a company to buy fixer-upper properties to sell for a profit. We bought and sold 16 houses in 2006, and most were short sales that we had negotiated.

In 2008, with some new partners we purchased a fixer-upper in Allentown, Pennsylvania that was listed with a successful real estate agent. The agent was impressed with how we had handled the short sale negotiation, and he asked if our company could negotiate with the banks for his other short sale listings. The agent mentioned that he and his staff did not have the time nor the expertise to negotiate with the mortgage lenders. We pondered how to make money on short sale negotiation, because in the past we made our money in buying short sale properties at a low price.

We started a program where we charged a flat fee up front to the seller in exchange for negotiating a short sale for them. We noticed that we could only charge so much, as most sellers were financially struggling.

After consulting with many attorneys, real estate brokers, and other advisors, we created a program that benefited everyone involved in the transaction. We did not charge the seller any fees. The buyer agreed to pay a fee at the settlement, and if the buyer did not purchase the property they owed us nothing. Therefore there was no risk to the seller or the buyer. Furthermore, our program provided a real estate attorney to represent the seller at no charge to them whatsoever. We noticed that most short sale sellers would not consult with a lawyer at all, as the traditional attorney model involves the client paying a retainer and an hourly legal fee. The short sale sellers just couldn't afford to consult an attorney via the traditional model. Our program gave the seller legal counsel from an attorney who specializes in short sales, and the mortgage lender would usually pay the attorney fee at the settlement.

At the end of 2014, after having closed hundreds of short sales through the years, I stepped away from the short sale company I co-founded to focus on running a large real estate brokerage in Pennsylvania. In 2015 I married my sweetheart Amira.

Even though I thought I was done with short sales, dozens of people – sellers, buyers, lawyers, brokers, negotiators, and investors – kept coming to me with questions about short sales. Realizing that there is a need in Pennsylvania for short sale insights, I decided I must publish this book. If this book can help prevent even just one foreclosure, then it will have been worth the effort.

Visit me at my website https://investandtransform.com/. You can email me at tai@investandtransform.com.

APPENDIX

Sample Hardship Letter

John Smith
Phone: XXX-555-1212

RE: SHORT SALE | LOAN NUMBERS XXXX AND XXXX

Dear [Lender]:

Please approve a short sale for my property located at XX XXXX Street in XXXX, Pennsylvania. I am dealing with a Distant Employment Transfer/Relocation from XXXX to hundreds of miles away in XXXX, XXXX. I am actively looking for a job in XXXX, yet I have not found one yet.

I consulted with a real estate broker who informed me that the fair market value of XX XXXX Street is about $50,000 to $60,000 less than the total balance of both mortgages. I could barely afford the payments for XXXX Street with my job in XXXX. There is no way I can pay for the home in XX and the one in Pennsylvania. I need to sell XX XXXX Street.

My savings are so low I can barely cover one month of expenses. Even if I rented my house to a tenant, it would be a negative cash flow situation. I can't seem to win. I am barely making my payments as it is. The broker I have hired has sold many short sales. I am confident that together we will find a solution.

Please approve the short sale for me and forgive the remaining debt.

Sincerely,

John Smith

Sample Hardship Letter

Jane Doe
XX XXXX Drive
XXXX, PA
Phone: XXX-555-5555

RE: SHORT SALE | LOAN NUMBER XXXXXXX

Dear [Lender]:

Please approve a short sale for me. I have breast cancer and receive chemotherapy treatments. I have fluid in my lungs and cough all the time. I was forced to move in with my son so he can help care for me.

I was self-employed, but I completely stopped working because I am so sick. I have no paystubs to provide. I have no profit and loss statement because I can no longer work. I am in pain a lot.

My property taxes are delinquent. My monthly bills keep getting higher and higher. The only money I have coming in is about $800 a month in public assistance. I cannot pay for the house any more.

I am struggling and I am scared. I need your help with allowing a short sale. I am trying to do the right thing. My friends tell me to declare bankruptcy, but I want to do a short sale. I have hired a real estate agent to sell the house. His name is XXX XXXXXX and his email address is XXX@XXXXX and his phone number is XXX-XXX-XXXX.

Sincerely,

Jane Doe

Letter to Servicer to Approve the Short Sale (It Worked!)

To: [Servicer]

From: XXXX, on behalf of John Doe

RE: LOAN # XXXXX | DELAY SHERIFF'S SALE TO AVOID LITIGATION

To Whom It May Concern:

Please delay the Sheriff's Sale of XX XXXX Drive in XXXX, Pennsylvania immediately. It is scheduled for XXX XX, XXXX. **Inform your investor that they may be damaged by attempting to continue with the foreclosure.**

Mr. Doe has consulted with his real estate attorney and bankruptcy attorney. **Mr. Doe intends to declare bankruptcy prior to the Sheriff's Sale if you do not take action now.** His real estate attorney also claims that [Servicer] has been negotiating in bad faith. The attorney may initiate legal action against [Servicer].

A substantial offer at fair market value was submitted on XXX XX, XXXX, and again on XXX XX, XXXX to [Servicer] negotiator XXX XXXX. Mr. XXXX has declined to review this offer by claiming a litany of reasons, such as stating that it is too close to the foreclosure sale date and that the offer is below fair market value.

Your investor will be damaged if you do not delay the Sheriff's Sale and consider the substantial offer we have submitted. Mr. Doe is prepared to take legal action today, which will delay the Sheriff's Sale for at least six months. Furthermore, the house may lose value during that time, and [Servicer] will have to start the foreclosure proceeding all over again. **Your investor will recover far more money now by having [Servicer] approve the short sale for a closing within days.**

Sincerely,

XXX XXXX
Senior Negotiator

Letter to Lender to Approve the Short Sale (It Worked!)

To: [Lender]

From: XXXX, on behalf of XXXX and XXXX XXXX

RE: LOAN # XXXX | LETTER OF EXPLANATION

To Whom It May Concern:

We respectfully request that you approve the short sale for XX XXX in XXXX, Pennsylvania for a sale price of $199,900 with a minimum acceptable net proceeds of $183,000. This is the highest and best offer that can be produced.

The parties have all made sacrifices, to include:
- The listing agent has cut thousands of dollars off of his commission.
- The seller's attorney has cut his fee by 60%.
- The selling agent has cut hundreds of dollars off of his commission.
- Instead of seller-paid closing costs of 6%, the buyer is procuring additional funds since they will only be allowed a 3% seller assist.
- The sellers have been paying to maintain the house despite their financial struggle.

This transaction was originally supposed to be settled on XXX XX, XXXX. Due to a host of delays, the seller allowed the buyer to move into the home until the short sale occurs. If you reject this short sale, then the buyer will not be able to purchase their dream home and the property will slide into foreclosure.

[Lender's] corporate values (attached) mention the use of "judgment and common sense," and state that [Lender] employees should "listen, treat people fairly, be inclusive, value different perspectives," and "care about individuals and their progress." If you approve this short sale, given the sacrifices of the parties, then you will be operating in accordance with your corporate values. You will be benefiting the community.

If you decline the short sale over a matter of a couple thousand dollars, then that means you are condemning the seller to a permanent foreclosure on their record, forcing the buyer out of their dream home, ensuring that the agents and attorney receive no compensation whatsoever for their efforts to help produce $183,000 for [Lender], and lowering home values even more for the community.

Your investor will recover far more money now by approving the short sale under the current conditions, and the closing will occur within days. Please approve this short sale as presented, even if an exception has to be made. **Your actions on this transaction will impact a lot of families.**

Sincerely,

XXX XXXX
Negotiator

Encl: [Lender] Values and Business Principles

Petition to a Motions Court Judge to Delay the Sheriff's Sale (It Worked!)

IN THE COURT OF COMMON PLEAS OF XXXX COUNTY, PENNSYLVANIA
CIVIL DIVISION

XXXX BANK	:		
Plaintiff	:		
vs.	:		
	:	No. XX-X-XXXX	
JOHN DOE, JANE DOE and	:		
UNITED STATES OF AMERICA	:		
	:		
Defendants	:		

DEFENDANT'S MOTION TO STAY SHERIFF'S SALE OF REAL PROPERTY SCHEDULED FOR FEBRUARY XX, 2XXX

AND NOW COMES, defendants John Doe and Jane Doe, by and through counsel, XXX XXX, Esq., and aver the following:

1. John Doe and Jane Doe (hereinafter "Mr. and Mrs. Doe") are the Defendants in this action.

2. Mr. and Mrs. Doe own the property located at XXX XXXX Drive, XXXX, Pennsylvania XXXXX.

3. Mr. and Mrs. Doe reside at the above-referenced address.

4. The Sheriff's Sale in this matter is currently scheduled for **February XX, 2XXX**.

5. On December 27, 2XXX Mr. and Mrs. Doe executed an Agreement of Sale for the said property for a purchase price of $XXX,XXXX with no mortgage contingency, as it is an all-cash, AS-IS offer. (Exhibit A – Agreement of Sale).

6. Said property has appraised for a value between $XXX,XXX and $XXX,XXX, an amount less than the current purchase price pursuant to the valid Agreement of Sale. (Exhibit B – Buyer's Appraisal and Plaintiff's Broker's Price Opinion).

7. With the current offer, Plaintiff stands to net an estimated 95% of its outstanding balance. (Exhibit C – Estimated HUD-1 Settlement Statement).

8. As an ancillary, yet critical, matter, said property is subject to an IRS tax lien, recorded in XXXX County at docket number XXXX-X-XXXX, that is being negotiated for release to facilitate the sale of the property.

9. Due to the federal government shutdown of 34 days, negotiations for the IRS lien release have been delayed at no fault of Mr. and Mrs. Doe.

10. Mr. and Mrs. Doe are XX years old and XX years old respectively, and in a dire financial situation.

11. Granting a stay of sheriff's sale would benefit all parties to this action by allowing closing of escrow for an above-value purchase price and a net proceed amount that would make Plaintiff almost completely whole.

WHEREFORE, Mr. and Mrs. Doe respectfully request that this Court grant a stay of the scheduled Sheriff's Sale scheduled for February XX, 2XXX or in the alternative grant a postponement of the Sheriff's Sale for a length of six (6) months to allow for negotiation of the short sale and closing of escrow.

Respectfully submitted,

By:_____

XXX XXX, Esquire
Attorney I.D. #
XX XXX Lane
XXX, PA XXXX
555-555-1212
Attorney for Defendants

<u>VERIFICATION</u>

The undersigned hereby states that the statements of fact in this motion are true and correct to the best of my information and belief. I understand that the statements herein are made subject to the penalties of 18 Pa.C.S.A. § 4904 relating to unsworn falsification to authorities.

_____   _____

John Doe   Date

_____   _____

Jane Doe   Date

IN THE COURT OF COMMON PLEAS OF XXXX COUNTY, PENNSYLVANIA
CIVIL DIVISION

XXXX BANK :
        Plaintiff   :

    vs.   :

                                              :   No. XX-X-XXX

JOHN DOE, JANE DOE and :
UNITED STATES OF AMERICA   :

                                          :

              Defendants   :

CERTIFICATE OF SERVICE

I, XXX XXX, Esq., do hereby certify that on this   day of February, 2XXX, I served a true and correct copy of the foregoing Defendant's Motion to Stay Sheriff's Sale of Real Property, on the person listed below, at the address listed below, via **facsimile :**

[BANK'S ATTORNEY]

XXX LAW FIRM

XX XXXX Street

XXX PA XXXXX

_____

IN THE COURT OF COMMON PLEAS OF XXXX COUNTY, PENNSYLVANIA
CIVIL DIVISION

XXXX BANK   :
       Plaintiff   :
   vs.   :
                       :   No. XX-X-XXX
JOHN DOE, JANE DOE and   :
UNITED STATES OF AMERICA   :
                       :
        Defendants   :

O R D E R

AND NOW this _____ day of _____, 20____, upon

Defendant's Motion to Stay Sheriff's Sale of Real Property, it is hereby ORDERED

and DECREED that the Sheriff's Sale is STAYED.

BY THE COURT:

_____

                                          J.

IN THE COURT OF COMMON PLEAS OF XXXX COUNTY, PENNSYLVANIA
CIVIL DIVISION

XXXX BANK   :
            Plaintiff   :
  vs.   :
                             :   No. XX-X-XXX

JOHN DOE, JANE DOE and   :
UNITED STATES OF AMERICA   :
                               :
         Defendants   :

ORDER

AND NOW this _____ day of _____, 20____, upon

Defendant's Motion to Stay Sheriff's Sale of Real Property, it is hereby ORDERED

and DECREED that the Sheriff's Sale is continued to the _____ day of

_____, 20___ at _____ _____.m., at the XXXX County

Courthouse, XXXXXX, Pennsylvania.

BY THE COURT:

_____

J.

GLOSSARY

Abandonment
Situation in which a homeowner leaves the house with no intention to return.

Accrued
Expenses incurred but not yet paid (i.e. accumulated mortgage interest or property taxes).

Addendum
Any written addition or change to a contract.

Agent Self-Initiation
Ability for an agent to begin the short sale offer process with at www.equator.com.

Appraisal or Appraised Value
A valuation report completed by a licensed, certified, and independent third party that estimates a property's fair market value. An appraiser, who views the property, evaluates its exterior and interior condition, and compares the property to other recently sold homes in the area with comparable features.

Approval Letter
The letter issued by the lender that authorizes the short sale of a property if certain terms and conditions are met.

Arms-Length Transaction
The sale of a property in which the buyer and the seller have no existing relationship and are acting in their own self-interest and are under no undue influence or pressure from other parties. As a result, the property is sold in the open market under the sale terms and conditions that typically prevail in the marketplace. This is the normal basis for deriving "fair market value" of a property. The opposite is a non-arms-length transaction, in which the buyer and seller are family members, friends, or business associates.

As-Is
Property sold in its current condition. Also referred to as As-Is, Where-Is.

Auction
The process of selling a property at a public sale to the highest bidder.

Authorization Letter

A form dated and signed by the borrower authorizing the lender to discuss personal information with a real estate professional or negotiator. The form specifically names the authorized third party and includes their contact information, the property address, and loan number.

Back on Market (BOM)

A property that was temporarily off the market, usually because a purchase offer was accepted, but the deal fell through and the property has been placed for sale once again.

Bank Walkaway

A situation where the lender decides not to foreclose on a delinquent borrower because the value of the property is deemed to be less than the cost of seizing it. The bank walks away from the collection of the delinquent loan.

Bankruptcy

A proceeding in a federal court that alters or eliminates one's obligations to repay some or all of their debts. Different chapters or types of bankruptcy exist.

Bankruptcy: Chapter 13

Involves a court-approved repayment plan. Debtors repay their debts over three to five years and must submit a plan to the court detailing how they propose to pay off the debts.

Bankruptcy: Chapter 7

A legal procedure that wipes out all allowable debts. It creates a bankruptcy estate out of the debtor's property, which may then be sold to pay off the debts.

Beneficiary

The lender in a deed of trust.

Broker's Price Opinion (BPO)

Estimated value of a property as determined by a real estate broker or other qualified individual or firm. A broker price opinion or comparable (or competitive) market analysis is based on the characteristics of the property being considered.

Buyer's Agent

The real estate licensee who represents the buyer in the real estate transaction. Also known as the Selling Agent.

Buyer's Closing Costs
Recurring or non-recurring costs typically paid by a buyer in a real estate transaction. In some cases, the seller may pay some of these costs for a buyer through what is known as a seller assist or seller-paid closing costs. Non-recurring costs are one-time costs such as escrow, title insurance, and loan fees. Recurring costs are those that do not end, such as property taxes and insurance.

Buyer Assist
Seller closing expenses that the buyer agrees to pay at settlement because neither the seller nor the seller's lender will pay for those expenses. This is common with short sales, as the buyer may have to pay some traditional seller costs that the seller cannot afford to pay themselves.

Cash Contribution
Cash contribution or a promissory note for future payment may be requested, depending on the lender and the borrower's financial situation. A contribution does not always mean that the remaining deficiency will be waived.

Certificate of Occupancy (CO)
A document issued by a local jurisdiction certifying that all building codes have been met and the property has been properly inspected by an inspector of the municipality.

Clear Title
Ownership in real estate that is marketable and/or free of liens or disputes.

Close of Escrow (COE)
The settlement, or closing, date.

Closing/Settlement
Process of finalizing a real estate transaction where final documents pertaining to the sale or purchase of a property are reviewed by the interested parties, signed as required, with money conveyed to complete the transaction.

Closing Costs
Costs or expenses associated with buying or selling real estate, including transfer taxes, real estate agent commissions, loan, title, appraisal, and/or attorney fees.

Cloud on Title
Defect in the title like a lien, claim, judgment or encumbrance that impairs the owner's ability to market the property.

Collateral
Asset like real estate or personal property pledged as security for a debt.

Conforming Mortgage
A mortgage loan that meets the lending standards of Fannie Mae and Freddie Mac, the two major entities that buy mortgages on the secondary market, helping ensure that primary lenders having sufficient funding to make new home loans.

Contingency
A legal requirement in a contract, often with a time limit, which must be fulfilled for the contract to remain valid. Buyers often include contingencies related to appraisal of the property, ability to obtain financing, approval of inspection results, and obtaining clear title to the property.

Cooperative Short Sale
Proactive approach whereby the short sale is initiated before an offer is made on the property. This is in contrast to a traditional short sale, which begins after a signed offer is received by the lender. The proactive approach allows the servicer to gather paperwork and required documents in advance. The servicer provides the homeowner with a suggested list price that is based on the current market value. Examples of a cooperative short sale include Home Affordable Foreclosure Alternatives (HAFA) and the Bank of America Cooperative Short Sale Program.

Counteroffer
Response to an original offer, rejecting or altering current terms, which can be presented by the seller or the buyer for rejection or acceptance. Amendments may include changes to the purchase price, the closing costs, and/or the settlement date.

Credit Report
A report compiled by a credit bureau that details credit history, credit inquiries, and facts about all accounts ever opened with respective to credit lines and on-time or late payment behavior used to evaluate credit risk.

Credit Score (FICO Score)
A three digit number between 450 and 850 calculated using a formula that indicates a borrower's ability to repay a loan based on the person's credit report

information, typically sourced from credit bureaus. FICO stands for Fair Isaac Corporation, which developed the scoring system.

Current Value
The value of a property at the time of appraisal.

Debt Forgiveness
When a lender agrees to accept less than the full balance of a loan as full and final satisfaction of the loan. The lender considers the borrower's debt obligation to be completed once they have received an agreed-upon amount.

Deed
A written instrument that when signed and delivered conveys title to or interest in real estate. Used in Pennsylvania.

Deed-in-Lieu of Foreclosure
A deed given by a borrower when in default to the lender to satisfy a debt and avoid foreclosure, per an agreement between the lender and borrower. Also called a "voluntary conveyance" or "friendly foreclosure."

Deed Package
The documents sent to the closing department by the closing company or the escrow company.

Deed of Reconveyance
An instrument that releases and discharges a deed of trust in some U.S. states, when the mortgage has been paid.

Deed of Trust or Trust Deed
A type of security instrument in some U.S. states conveying title in trust to a third party covering a particular piece of property.

Default
Situation when the borrower does not meet his or her legal obligations according to the loan terms. Most defaults are triggered by payments more than 30 days late.

Defaulted Loan
The status of a loan, as determined by the lender, indicating that the borrower has missed making one or more regular payments or failed to meet some other obligation.

Deficiency

The remaining unpaid balance on a mortgage after a foreclosure sale, a short sale, or in some cases a deed-in-lieu of foreclosure.

Deficiency Balance

Amount left over when the money realized from the sale of a distressed property is insufficient to pay off the full loan amount.

Deficiency Judgment

A judgment obtained after a distressed sale or conveyance that requires the borrower to pay the remaining balance due on the loan. Lenders can pursue the remaining deficiency in Pennsylvania if they initiate the lawsuit within six months after the sale.

Delinquent

Failure to make payments on time.

Delinquent Mortgage

A mortgage for which the borrower has failed to make payments as required in the loan documents. If the borrower can't bring the payments current within a certain time period, the lender may initialize foreclosure proceedings.

Demand Letter or Letter of Demand (LOD) or Breach Letter

Notice to the borrower that he or she is has violated the terms of a mortgage note.

Demand

Request for payoff; a note payable on demand of the holder.

Down Payment

Cash paid toward the purchase of a home to make up the difference between the purchase price and the mortgage loan.

Dual Agent

A real estate agent who represents both the buyer and the seller in the same transaction. It may also refer to a real estate agency that represents both parties, even if the agents are different. Dual agency is legal in Pennsylvania if disclosed and if permitted by the Broker of Record.

Dual Tracking
A situation where a mortgage lender or servicer considers a delinquent borrower for an alternative to foreclosure (loan modification, short sale, forbearance plan, or deed-in-lieu of foreclosure) while at the same time trying to repossess the property through foreclosure.

Earnest Money Deposit (EMD)
A deposit made by the potential homebuyer to show that he or she is serious about buying the house. Also known as a good faith deposit.

Equator
The online short sale interface used by some major banks, including Bank of America, J.P. Morgan Chase, Wells Fargo, Ally, America's Servicing Company, Carrington, Mr. Cooper (Nationstar), and others. It is accessed at www.equator.com.

Equity
The monetary value of a property beyond what is owed on the loan(s) against it.

Escrow
The holding of assets by a third party, such as a lender, title agent, or attorney. An escrow account is one that is established to hold separate funds for the purpose of paying bills such as homeowner's insurance and property taxes.

Estoppel
A legal restraint that stops or prevents a person from contradicting or reneging on their previous position or previous assertions or commitments.

Estoppel Certificate
Instrument executed by the mortgagor that sets forth the status of and balance due on the mortgage as of the date of certificate execution.

Eviction
A legal proceeding to recover possession of real property from the tenant.

Extension of Time Agreement
An agreement typically in writing that gives additional time to pay an obligation.

Executive Review
In a short sale with unique circumstances, the lender may require a special decision from high level executives.

Fair Credit Reporting Act
A federal law that regulates the collection, dissemination, and use of consumer information, including consumer credit information.

Fair Market Value (FMV)
The most likely sales price of a property within a specific amount of time with proper marketing. An appraised value is an estimate of the current fair market value. Offers are compared to an independent assessment of the home's current market value.

Fannie Mae (FNMA)
Federal National Mortgage Association (FNMA) commonly known as Fannie Mae is a federally chartered corporation that buys mortgages that meet its standards from mortgage lenders then pools them and sells them as mortgage-backed securities to investors on the open market. Fannie guarantees the monthly principal and interest payments on the mortgage-backed securities it issues.

Federal Housing Administration (FHA)
Federal agency that provides mortgage insurance for residential loans with very low down payments. Is a part of the Department of Housing and Urban Development (HUD). The borrower pays the insurance premium and the lender is the beneficiary. In the event of borrower default, FHA pays the lender an amount covering some or all of the outstanding loan balance.

Financials
Income- and asset-related documents that are required to help determine if a short sale will be approved. Financial documents may include the last two years' worth of tax returns, two months of bank statements, and last pay stubs from the last two pay periods.

First Mortgage
A mortgage that has priority over all mortgages and liens except those imposed by law.

Forbearance
A postponement of loan payments, granted by a lender or creditor, for a temporary period of time. This is done to give the borrower time to make up for overdue payments.

Force Placed Insurance, or Forced Placed Insurance

Insurance purchased by a bank or creditor on an uninsured debtor's behalf. The premium is paid by the lender and typically added to the principal balance.

Foreclosure

Foreclosure is a legal procedure in which property pledged as security is sold to satisfy the debt. A mortgage lender's rights can be enforced through foreclosure if the borrower defaults on mortgage payments or fails to fulfill any of the other obligations in the mortgage. There are two types of foreclosure: judicial foreclosure, which is handled as a civil lawsuit and conducted under the supervision of the court; and non-judicial foreclosure, which does not require formal court proceedings and is overseen by a trustee selected by the lender.

Foreclosure Hold

The postponement of a property foreclosure, typically by a lender.

Freddie Mac (FHLMC)

Federal Home Loan Mortgage Corporation commonly known as Freddie Mac is a quasi-governmental agency that purchases conventional mortgages from insured depository institutions and HUD- approved mortgage bankers.

Government-Sponsored Enterprise (GSE)

A collection of financial services corporations formed by Congress to reduce interest rates for farmers and homeowners. Examples include Fannie Mae and Freddie Mac.

Hardship

The documented circumstances that have caused the homeowner to default on the mortgage and seek a short sale. The hardship documentation must be signed by the person experiencing the hardship. Hardships include illness of the borrower, divorce, and loss of income.

Hardship Letter

A lender required letter written by a borrower applying for a short sale that describes why the borrower can't pay his or her mortgage payments.

Hazard Insurance

Is insurance protection for the borrower and lender against property loss due to fire, wind or natural hazards.

Held for Investment
A loan retained for investment purposes. A mortgage loan shall not be classified as HFI unless the mortgage banker has both the intent and the ability to hold the loan for the foreseeable future or until maturity.

Home Affordable Foreclosure Alternatives (HAFA) Short Sale
Part of the Federal Government's Making Home Affordable (MHA) program, the Home Affordable Foreclosure Alternatives (HAFA) program was developed to give homeowners a way to settle their mortgage debt without going through a foreclosure. The program offers a streamlined method for selling a residential property via a short sale. The program also offers a deed-in-lieu option. Under the HAFA program, homeowners who sell their home in a short sale or sign it over in a deed-in-lieu are offered incentives to help them relocate.

Home Affordable Modification Program (HAMP)
As part of the federal government's Making Home Affordable program, HAMP is a loan modification program designed to reduce at-risk borrowers' monthly mortgage payments.

Home Equity Line of Credit (HELOC)
Normally a junior or secondary mortgage loan.

Home Equity Installment Loan (HEIL)
A line of credit (loan) that is secured by the equity in a property.

Home Warranty/Home Protection Plan (HW/HPP)
A type of insurance that covers repairs to specified parts of a house for a specific period of time. The builder or the property seller may provide it as a condition of the sale, but homeowners can also purchase it.

HUD-1 Settlement Statement
A closing document that provides an itemized list of the credits and charges, for both the buyer and the seller, based on the contract terms. The HUD-1 statement is also known as the "closing statement" or "settlement sheet."

Imminent Default
Imminent default is a term that refers to a borrower who is current on his or her mortgage loan but is at risk of not being able to continue to pay the monthly home loan payments due to a financial hardship or an upcoming interest rate increase or payment reset that will cause the monthly payments to become unaffordable.

Initial Services (IS)
Securing the property by re-keying, placing a lockbox on the real estate-owned (REO) property, boarding up windows or doors if needed, and removing any identified debris from the interior and the exterior of property. When initial services have been completed, the property is considered "sales clean."

Inspection Period
A specific period of time for the buyer, the buyer's agent, and inspectors to examine a property prior to closing.

Installment Account
Is an account that has a set regular payment, typically every month.

Instrument
A legal written document.

Investor
The person or institution who owns the mortgages or mortgage-backed securities, providing the funds that the homeowner is able to borrow to purchase a property. Each investor can set different policies. Many loans have multiple investors.

Investor Decision
When a homeowner wants to sell a property for less than what is owed on the mortgage, the servicer must obtain approval from the owner of the mortgage or mortgage-backed securities. That owner's "yes" or "no" response to this short sale proposal is the investor decision.

IRS Publication 982
IRS form that under certain circumstances may exclude the discharge of certain debt (like mortgage debt) from income, thereby eliminating tax consequences from doing a short sale.

Judgment
The financial decision of a court resolving a dispute and determining the rights and obligations of parties.

Judicial Foreclosure
A type of foreclosure proceeding used in some U.S. states, including Pennsylvania, that is handled as a civil lawsuit in a court of law.

Junior Mortgage
A mortgage that takes a subordinate position to another loan.

Lender
Party from whom something of value, typically money, is borrowed.

Lender-approved Short Sale
Conducting a short sale with the lender agreeing to accept the proceeds of the sale and "forgive" the remaining amount of mortgage owed.

Loan Term
The period of time over which a loan must be repaid, such as 15 or 30 years.

Lien
A legal claim of money against a property, wherein the value of the property is used as security in repayment of a debt. A lien is a defect on the title and needs to be settled before transfer of ownership. Lien priority is generally established by the order in which the liens were recorded:

Senior lien: Usually a first mortgage.

Junior lien: Usually a mortgage loan, home equity loan or line of credit. Junior liens may also include homeowner association fees, taxes, medical fees, child support, mechanic's liens and judgments.

Judgment lien: A legal order recorded against a property. When a creditor sues on a debt, the creditor may obtain a judgment requiring debt repayment, which may be attached as a property lien on a piece of property. A judgment is entered and recorded with the county recorder and often becomes a general lien on the property.

Lienholder
A person or corporation with a financial interest in a property or who places a lien against a piece of property because of non-payment of a debt.

Lien Release
Written report of the settlement of a lien. It is recorded in the public record as evidence of payment. The homeowner and listing agent must identify all liens and seek release.

Lien Waiver
A document that releases a homeowner (or other consumer) from any further obligation for payment of a debt once it has been paid in full. Lien waivers typically are used by homeowners who hire a contractor to provide work and materials to prevent any subcontractors or suppliers of materials from filing a lien against the homeowner for nonpayment.

Lis Pendens
A Latin phrase meaning "suit pending"; a formal notice that starts the foreclosure process in some U.S. states.

Listing Agent
The real estate agent who works for the seller to market and sell their property.

Listing Agreement or Listing Contract
A contract between a seller and a real estate professional to market and sell a property. A listing agreement obligates the real estate licensee to seek qualified buyers, report all purchase offers, and help negotiate the highest possible price and most favorable terms for the property seller.

Listing Office Commission (LOC)
Brokerage commission paid by the seller to a real estate broker to compensate the broker(s) involved in the sale for their services in marketing the property, finding a buyer, and assisting in the negotiations. Brokerage commissions are usually computed as a percentage of the sale price and are established in a listing agreement between the seller and the listing broker.

Loan
A verbal or written contract in which a borrower agrees to repay a specified sum of money given by a lender under specific terms and conditions, usually with interest.

Loan Reset
A situation where the mortgage lender agrees to substantially change the terms of a loan or eliminates a loan obligation, after the borrower successfully alleges that the origination of the loan violated certain rules or laws.

Loan Modification/Underwater
Is a procedure in which a loan's terms, such as the interest rate, monthly payment or term are altered with the approval of a lender.

Loan Servicer
The company that collects monthly mortgage payments and disperses property taxes and insurance payments. Loan servicers also monitor nonperforming loans, contact delinquent borrowers, and notify insurers and investors of potential problems. Loan servicers may be the lender or a specialized company that just handles loan servicing under contract with the lender or the investor who owns the loan.

Lockout
A scheduled meeting at the subject property with the local sheriff to execute a writ of possession and forcibly remove the occupants.

Loss Mitigation
The process of a homeowner and a servicer working together to come up with a solution for avoiding foreclosure when possible. Includes home-retention options, as well as short sale or deed-in-lieu of foreclosure options.

Material Fact
Includes information about a property that should be disclosed to a property buyer. It is something that would negatively affect the value of the property and/or harm people on the premises. A material fact may influence a buyer's decision to purchase property or negatively impact the buyer's decision. It might also alter the price and terms a buyer is willing to pay. Also known as a Material Defect.

Mechanic's Lien
A lien on real estate, created by operation of law, that secures the payment of debts due to persons who perform labor or services or furnish materials incident to the construction of buildings and improvements on the real estate.

MI Company
A mortgage insurance company that issues private mortgage insurance (PMI).

Modification
A change to the original terms of the loan. Loan modifications could include lowering the interest rate, extending the term or maturity date of the loan, moving from an adjustable to a fixed-rate loan, deferring some portion of the unpaid principal balance to the end of the loan, and/or forgiving some portion of the unpaid principal balance.

Moral Hazard
Occurs when a party insulated from risk behaves differently than it would behave if it were fully exposed to the risk.

Mortgage
A legal document giving a lender a lien on real estate to secure repayment of a loan. Mortgage loans generally run from 10 to 30 years, after which the loan is required to be paid off. Also called deed of trust and/or security deed.

Mortgage Insurance (MI)
A policy that protects lenders against some or most of the losses that can occur when a borrower defaults on a mortgage loan. Mortgage insurance is required primarily for borrowers with a down payment of less than 20% of the home's purchase price. The cost of mortgage insurance is usually added to the monthly payment. Mortgage insurance is maintained on conventional loans until the outstanding amount of the loan is less than 80% of the value of the house or for a set period (seven years is common). Mortgage insurance also is available through a government agency, such as the Federal Housing Administration (FHA) or through companies (private mortgage insurance or PMI). A short sale will often require the mortgage insurer's approval.

Multiple Listing Service (MLS)
A database of information on properties for sale that is accessible to all subscribing real estate brokers and their agents.

Natural Hazard Disclosure (NHD)
The Natural Hazards Disclosure Act of California, effective June 1, 1998 (as amended June 9, 1998), requires that sellers of real property and their agent provide any prospective buyer with a Natural Hazard Disclosure Statement when the property being sold lies within one or more state-mapped hazard areas.

Negative Equity
When the fair market value of a property is less than the outstanding balance of the loan(s) it secures. Commonly referred to as being "under water" or "upside down" on a house.

Neighborhood Assistance Corporation of America (NACA)
A nonprofit community advocacy and homeownership organization with the primary goal of building strong, healthy neighborhoods in urban and rural areas nationwide through affordable homeownership.

Neighborhood Stabilization Program (NSP)
A program established in 2008 by the Department of Housing and Urban Development (HUD) to stabilize communities that have suffered from foreclosures and abandonment. Through the purchase and redevelopment of foreclosed and abandoned homes and residential properties, the goal of the program is being realized.

Non-Arms-Length Transaction
Sale of a property that involves a buyer and a seller who have a relationship (family members, business associates, friends, or landlord/tenant). Because of this relationship, there may be no competitive offers received on the property. As a result, the selling price and the terms and conditions of the transaction are not subject to prevailing marketplace dynamics and may not represent "fair market value." The opposite is an arms-length transaction.

Non-Purchase Money Loan
A loan that was not used to purchase a property such as home equity line of credit (HELOC) or a loan used to refinance an existing loan.

Non-Judicial Foreclosure
In a deed of trust, if the borrower defaults on the loan, the trustee has the right to foreclose on and transfer title to the lender or sell the property to pay the lender from the proceeds. Because a court order is not required, this process is generally more expedient and less costly than judicial foreclosure.

Non-Performing Asset
An asset that does not produce money for the owner.

Notice of Default (NOD)
A written document that gives constructive notice of a trustor's failure to perform his obligation under a deed of trust. This document does not require the acknowledgment of a notary public and must be recorded.

Offer
Indication of a potential willing and able buyer's intention to enter into a contract to buy a property at a specific price. The offer is generally put forth in writing.

Partial Claim
A no-interest or low-interest loan given by a lender to help pay back any missing or partial mortgage payments and default-related fees. This is a one-time only loan. The partial claim loan is paid back when the mortgage loan is paid off.

Performing Loan
Is a loan whose interest payments are current and paid up to date.

Piggyback Loan
A second mortgage "piggybacked" onto a first mortgage used in lieu of mortgage insurance.

Postponement Request
A request submitted by the seller and/or their short sale negotiator to the lender, asking to delay the foreclosure sale. In some cases, the lender may agree to delay a foreclosure sale to allow a short sale to be considered.

Power Of Attorney (POA)
A legal document allowing one person to act in a legal matter on another's behalf in financial or real estate transactions.

Pre-foreclosure Sale
A property in a pre-foreclosure status means that the underlying mortgage loan is delinquent but a foreclosure sale has not yet occurred. A pre-foreclosure sale means that the sale occurred before the lender foreclosed.

Preliminary Net Sheet
An estimate of net proceeds from sale with expenses, including unpaid loan balances and fees, subtracted from the sales price. It may be a preliminary HUD-1 Settlement Statement.

Prequalification Letter
A lender's conditional agreement to lend a specific amount on specific terms to a homebuyer. Lenders may require that all potential buyers be prequalified by a mortgage loan originator. While all offers will be presented to the seller, the lender will not accept an offer if the buyer is unwilling to produce a lender prequalification letter or proof of funds.

Principal Balance
The amount owed on a loan before interest and fees.

Principal Extinguishment
A negotiated agreement between a lender and a borrower whereby the lender agrees to release all of the remaining debt and satisfy the mortgage lien without expectation of receiving any additional money.

Principal Reduction
A negotiated agreement between a lender and a borrower whereby the lender agrees to remove some of the underlying debt, with the borrower responsible for the remainder.

Private Mortgage Insurance (PMI)
A privately owned company that offers standard and special affordable mortgage insurance programs for qualified borrowers with down payments of less than 20% of a purchase price. A short sale will often require the mortgage insurer's approval.

Proceeds
In terms of a home sale, the amount of money left after all other debts and obligations related to the sale have been paid.

Profit & Loss Statement (P&L)
Financial statement that shows a company or individual's income and expenses. Lenders often require self-employed borrowers applying for a short sale to submit a P&L as a substitute for pay stubs.

Promissory Note
A written pledge for future payment of a loan. This may be requested, depending on the investor and homeowner's financial situation.

Proposed Close of Escrow
The projected close of escrow date, or the day the property is projected to close escrow or change title from the old owner to the new owner.

Public Auction or Step Sale or Sheriff's Sale
In foreclosure proceedings, when a property is sold at auction "on the courthouse steps."

Purchase Money Mortgage
A loan that was used to purchase a property.

Real Estate Owned (REO)
A property owned by a bank after the property has been foreclosed.

Reconciled Value
A value check that bank negotiators may order from the appraiser used by the lender or a different evaluator. This includes a review of the last appraisal with a current broker price opinion (BPO) from the agent (must be less than 30 days old) in order to update a current market value for the property. Once received, this value is good for up to 90 days and supersedes the original appraisal for marketing purposes.

Redemption
Is the right of a borrower to pay off a mortgage following a default by paying the amount due to the lender, along with certain other costs.

Redemption Period
Time period in a foreclosure that a borrower who is in default cannot be evicted or be divested of his legal title. This time period allows the borrower to repay his debt in full.

Reinstatement
Occurs when the property owner pays off the amount in default to bring the loan payments current in order to stop the foreclosure process and return to the original terms of a loan.

Request For Approval of Short Sale (RASS)
Letter supplied by the servicer and issued to the homeowner that illustrates guidelines applying to the HAFA program.

Return on Investment (ROI)
A performance measure used to evaluate the efficiency of an investment or to compare the efficiency of a number of different investments. To calculate ROI, the benefit (return) of an investment is divided by the cost of the investment; the result is expressed as a percentage or a ratio.

Revolving Account
Is an account created by a lender to represent debts where the outstanding balance does not have to be paid in full every month by the borrower to the lender.

Sales Clean
Getting the property ready for market; cleaning up the asset.

Sales Comparables (aka comps, comparables, sale comps)
Data regarding sales of recently sold properties similar in condition, style, size and location to a property being evaluated to determine its fair market value.

Sales Contract (aka Purchase Contract or Agreement of Sale)
A contract signed by a buyer and seller detailing the terms of a property purchase.

Second Mortgage / Second Lien
The traditional term for a home equity loan or line of credit because it is generally a subordinate lien and not a first mortgage, which usually is made to purchase the home.

Secure
Securing the property by re-keying, placing a lockbox on the property and/or boarding up windows or doors.

Seller's Concession or Seller's Assist
An agreement between buyer and seller normally written into a sales contract that gives the buyer a credit toward the purchase of a property. Also known as Seller Paid Closing Costs.

Selling Agent
The real estate agent representing the buyer. Also known as the Buyer's Agent.

Selling Office Commission (SOC)
Brokerage commission, paid by the seller to a real estate broker to compensate the broker(s) involved in the sale for their services in marketing the property, finding a buyer and assisting in the negotiations. Brokerage commissions are usually computed as a percentage of the sale price and are established in a listing agreement between the seller and the listing broker.

Senior Mortgage
First mortgage on a property, payment of which takes priority over the other (junior) mortgage(s) on the same property.

Servicer
An organization that collects principal and interest payments from borrowers and manages borrowers' tax and insurance escrow accounts. Many short sales negotiations go through servicers.

Servicing
The collection of mortgage payments from borrowers and related responsibilities of a loan server.

Short Sale or Short Pay or Payoff
A commonly used alternative to a foreclosure when the property is worth less than what is owed. In a short sale, the lender agrees to accept an amount less than what is actually owed on the loan based on a showing of financial hardship or other stipulations.

Short Sale Agreement (SSA)
The short sale approval letter issued by the lender.

Short Sale Package
Forms and instructions provided by a lender to a borrower interested in winning the lender's approval for a short sale. Also, the collection of documents -- including financial statements, hardship letter, sales contract, etc. -- submitted to a lender as a request for short-sale approval.

Short Sale Processing System
Technology that is used to process, track and communicate details of a short sale transaction. Equator and Short Sale Commander are examples of short sale processing systems.

Short Sale Specialist or Negotiator
Lender's associate who works in the Short Sale Department. This specialist is also known as a Negotiator and/or Closing Negotiator. The Short Sale Specialist is responsible for mitigating loss for the investor by negotiating the short sale purchase offer submitted by the seller's agent. The Negotiator is the mediator between the distressed homeowner and the investor, working to arrive at a selling price that will be acceptable to all parties. This specialist will communicate the investor's decision to the agent. In addition, the Short Sale Specialist negotiates closing costs, determining which items will be paid by whom. Can also refer to a representative for the seller.

Status Conference
A meeting or hearing called by a judge in judicial states whereby the delinquent borrower and the lender's attorney are asked to meet so the judge can decide whether to give the borrower time to explore an alternative to foreclosure or to allow the foreclosure lawsuit to proceed. Also known as a conciliation conference.

Strategic Default
The decision by a borrower to stop making payments on a debt despite having the financial ability to make the payments.

Straw Buyers
Submitting an offer into the system using a "pretend/fake buyer." Straw buyers can also conceal the identity of the real buyer.

Subordination
A clause in an agreement which states that the current claim on any debts will take priority over any other claims formed in other agreements made in the future. Subordination is the act of yielding priority. For example, real estate taxes and municipal liens normally subordinate mortgage liens which incentivizes primary lienholders to pay property taxes when a borrower stops paying his mortgage.

Task
An assignment in the short sale processing system that must be completed in order to move forward in the short sale process. A task can be assigned to a Short Sale Specialist and to the authorized third party (usually the seller's agent).

Tax Lien
Is a lien on real estate that may be foreclosed for nonpayment in favor of a state or local government.

Title
Legal evidence of right of ownership of real property (real estate).
Title Company
Examines property title and issues title insurance.

Title Insurance
Insurance issued against the loss or damage from defects of title to real property.

Title Report
The written analysis of the status of title to real estate, including a property description, names of titleholders and how title is held (joint tenancy, etc.), tax rate, encumbrances (mortgages, liens, deeds of trusts, recorded judgments) and real property taxes due.

Title Search
A search performed within public records to determine ownership as well as claims or liens against a property.

Traditional Short Sale
Reactive approach in which the short sale negotiation is begun after a signed offer is received by the bank. (This is in contrast to a cooperative short sale or HAFA, a proactive approach in which the short sale is initiated before an offer is made on the property.)

Transfer Fees (TF)
Money paid to the county and/or state when the property is sold.

Trash Out
Removing debris and personal property from the asset and getting it into broom-swept condition inside and out.

Trustor
The borrower in a deed of trust.

Underwater or Upside Down
When the mortgage loan balance is greater than the home's value.

Unsecured Loan
A loan that is not secured by a lien.

Valuation
Process to determine what a property is worth, usually via an appraisal or Broker's Price Opinion.

Wire Confirmation
A document verifying that funds were wired to the appropriate institution. The wire confirmation will reflect the date, time, amount sent, the account the funds were wired to, and the loan number that the funds are to be applied to. The Closing

Negotiator will provide the wiring information at the time he/she approves the preliminary final Settlement Statement; this allows the title company to know where to wire the funds after closing.

Worksheet
The platform used in the short sale processing system where the selling agent enters all items from the Settlement Statement that are to be included for approval. This information may then be negotiated by the Short Sale Specialist. Agreement must be reached on which items to include in the worksheet before the short sale process can move forward. This agreement does not apply approval of the proposed short sale.

ABOUT THE AUTHOR

Tai A. DeSa has devoted much of his real estate career to helping people avoid foreclosure and negotiate a short sale with their mortgage lender.

DeSa grew up in Stroudsburg, Pennsylvania, the oldest of 11 children. He was the valedictorian of the Class of 1993 at Notre Dame High School in East Stroudsburg. He then earned a Bachelor of Science in Economics from The Wharton School at the University of Pennsylvania in 1997.

After graduating college, DeSa joined the United States Navy. He completed Officer Candidate School and was commissioned as an officer in January 1998. He served on the aircraft carrier USS Kitty Hawk, completing multiple deployments in the Arabian Gulf and Pacific Ocean. DeSa then served with the Defense Intelligence Agency Directorate of Operations, conducting operations in Asia and Eastern Europe. He later served with the Navy's Fifth Fleet headquarters for the first year of the Iraq War.

DeSa then left the Navy to become a full-time real estate investor in 2004. In late 2005, DeSa co-founded a short sale negotiation company that operated in multiple states. In 2008, DeSa decided to obtain a real estate license and became a real estate broker the following year. In 2015, DeSa stepped out of the short sale firm and into a role leading a large real estate brokerage. DeSa is now a broker in Pennsylvania and Tennessee. He coaches and consults real estate investors and people involved in short sales.

DeSa is married to his wife Amira, and they are thrilled to be raising their twin daughters Alexis and Ashley.

ACKNOWLEDGEMENTS

I would like to first and foremost thank my beautiful wife Amira. I am grateful for my twin daughters Alexis and Ashley. And of course, thank you to my parents who helped influence me to be the person I am today. Thank you to my siblings, Sa, Truc, Tri, Van, Tam, Trinh, Thanh, Trung, Hong, and Thang.

To my son, Creed Daniel DeSa, who is with Jesus in Heaven.

The Charity of Choice for me is KW Cares. Go to https://www.kwcares.org/ for more information.

www.ingramcontent.com/pod-product-compliance
Lightning Source LLC
Chambersburg PA
CBHW030625220526
45463CB00004B/1414